THE
MICROLIGHT
PILOT'S
HANDBOOK

To
Flt Lt Norman 'Invader' Currell DFC
My flying mentor in World War II

BRIAN COSGROVE

THE MICROLIGHT PILOT'S HANDBOOK

Suitable for all pilots of microlight,
light aircraft and gliders

Acknowledgements:
S. Weston – (Artwork)
J. Doswell

Airlife
England

By the same Author – *Microlight Aircraft and the Air*
Eyewitness Series – 'Weather'
The World of Weather
Pilot's Weather

Copyright © Brian Cosgrove 1998

ISBN 1 84037 068 8

First edition published 1986
by Airlife Publishing Ltd

This 6th revised edition published 1998

Fourth impression 2001

Printed in England by Livesey Ltd, Shrewsbury.

Airlife Publishing Ltd

101 Longden Road, Shrewsbury SY3 9EB, England
Email: airlife@airlifebooks.com
Website: www.airlifebooks.com

Contents

The Author

From designing, building and flying model aircraft in the 1930s through service with the Air Defence Cadet Corps, Air Training Corps and Royal Air Force in the 1940s, the author has always had an affinity for aeroplanes since a first flight at the age of seven. 1942/43 saw his involvement as a pupil in the opening days of A.T.C. gliding where solo training in open primary types was the norm – shades of microlights to come 40 years later.

After wartime service with the R.A.F. in the U.K. and Far East as a Meteorologist on the ground and in the air, the early post war years were spent as a gliding instructor culminating in an 'A' Star Category in both solo and dual methods of training.

Predicting that total freedom for microlighting would be short-lived, work began on ideas for control on a self-regulatory basis. Reading matter for ground studies appeared in the form of *Microlight Aircraft in the Air*.

When parliamentary pressure on the CAA to legislate on microlights overtook the aspirations of self regulation, effort was then channelled into ensuring that such legislation would be meaningful. A start was made in preparing future pilot licence examinations specific to microlights. These were accepted by the CAA and a rapport was established which was to grow over future years.

By then a BMAA Council member, negotiations continued with the CAA on many aspects of pilot licensing, instructor rating until involvement became full-time as Secretary of the BMAA. Some months later as Chief Executive, airworthiness procedures were set up and safeguards put in place for existing aeroplanes threatened with grounding by airworthiness standards yet to be introduced.

After retiring as Chief Executive of the BMAA in May 1993, work for the Association continued on a consultancy basis.

The author was awarded the Ashley Doubtfire Trophy in 1985 for Services to Microlight Aviation and in 1990 was elected a Freeman of the Guild of Air Pilots and Air Navigators and currently serves as a member of the Guild's Education and Training Committee. In 1993 came election as a Fellow of the Royal Meteorological Society and the award of an MBE in the Queen's Birthday Honours List.

Introduction

Although the microlight may make satisfying that 'dream' to fly much closer than it has ever been, the knowledge to do so remains similar in many aspects to the standards required for flying conventional light aeroplanes. In fact it could be quite justifiably argued that the standards must be greater in some respects in view of the ordinary fields from which the microlight can operate.

The aim of this book is not just to prepare you for passing the PPL (A) Microlight examinations as an end in itself, but to provide you with a real understanding and recognition of those factors which influence safe flight for you and passengers who will fly with you in the future – be it in a microlight or in any other form of aircraft. The principles are the same.

There are eight broad aspects with which you must concern yourself.

Principles of Flight	– Why your aeroplane can fly
Power and Ancillaries	– How to ensure it stays flying
Meteorology	– The environment in which you fly
Air Law	– The rules to be obeyed when you fly
Human Performance Limitations	– Your mind and body as you fly
Basic Flight Instruments	– What happens as you fly
Navigation	– Planning your way before you fly
Map Reading	– Finding your way as you fly

This sixth edition of the book continues to fulfil the aim to update where necessary. Particular attention is still paid to those aspects of Air Law where the microlight aeroplane may be operating under exemptions from the law laid down in the Air Navigation Order. Such exemptions are unlikely to be covered in other publications on air law but they still require legal compliance and the pilot must have knowledge of them.

An additional chapter has been added on Foot Launched Powered Flying Machines (FLPFM) – a new way to fly which has joined our family.

Throughout the book, where information is considered to be of interest, but not necessarily essential, the text is marked * at the start and ** at the end.

As before, the subject of how to fly the aeroplane has been left where it belongs – in the hands of your flying instructor.

However, digest the contents presented to you herein and you and your instructor will have a much easier ride.

Brian Cosgrove

Principles of Flight

Principles of Flight

Learning to fly a microlight relates to handling the various controls and becoming aware of their effect on your flight path. However, it is not enough to know what these effects are; there must be awareness of why the effects take place and in fact why the aircraft can fly at all.

This chapter covers a variety of microlight types and control systems some of which are only relevant to earlier machines no longer in production. This content has not been removed, as the days of innovation are not yet dead and who knows – the principles involved may yet re-appear with new designs.

The Aerofoil

Flight is possible because a wing can generate lift and it does so in two ways.
- By the angle at which it meets the **Airflow** – known as the **Angle of Attack** in relation to the chord line of the wing.
- By the shape of the wing section from front to back – **Leading Edge** to **Trailing Edge**. This shape is known as the **Aerofoil Section** and is generally flattish on the bottom and curved on the top. This curve is known as **Camber** and later you will see how camber contributes around two-thirds of the total lift produced. The **Datum Line** through an aerofoil section is known as the **Chord Line**.

Basic terms in **bold** above are to be seen in Fig. 1.

Fig.1

Chord Line · Leading Edge · Camber · Aerofoil Section · Trailing Edge · Angle of Attack · Airflow

Airspeed

A cambered wing set at an angle of attack will not in itself create lift. When you watch an aircraft take off you will see that at first it accelerates along the ground until at a particular point it parts company with 'mother earth' and flies.

What happens is this. The forward movement causes air to flow over the wing and it is this flow of air called **Airspeed** that produces the lift. The greater the airspeed the greater is the lift that the wing will generate.

When the airspeed is sufficient to produce enough lift for flight the aircraft is said to have reached **Flying Speed**.

Angle of Attack

Consider now the angle of attack and its contribution to lift. As the airflow meets the wing leading edge it divides to pass under and over the aerofoil.

Fig.2

In Fig.2 above you can see how the air passing underneath is deflected downwards. This in turn creates an opposite effect in that the aerofoil is pushed up. In fact it creates one-third of total lift.

Take a piece of card and swing it around at arms length making sure that you hold it at an angle as you do so. You will find that the card will try to lift out of your hand and the faster you swing it the more it tries to rise.

The airflow deflected down by the Angle of Attack produces a **Resultant** upward force. (Fig.3.)

Resultant

Fig.3

Relative
Airflow

Camber

Next let us consider the contribution made to total lift by camber.

The air moving over the top cambered surface has further to travel to meet up with the air passing underneath. If both are to meet at the same time at the trailing edge (which they must do) then the air travelling over the cambered top has to travel faster to keep up.

Picture a river flowing sedately along being suddenly faced with a restriction. The given amount of water speeds up in order to pass through the restriction without causing a build up behind. It will be going at its fastest at the narrowest point.

A scientist called Bernoulli found that the faster a fluid went through such a restriction then the less became the pressure it exerted on the sides of that restriction. (Fig.4).

Fig.4

Fluid Flow

Normal → | Faster → | Fastest → | Less Fast → | Normal →

Least

Normal | Less | Less | Normal

Pressure on side

Look carefully at the shape of the sides of the restriction. Remove one side, say the top one, and you will see a curved surface closely resembling the cambered surface of an aerofoil.

Now air behaves as a fluid and as it speeds up over the camber the pressure exerted on that top surface will decrease as per Bernoulli's findings.

Naturally if pressure on the top decreases it makes pressure below become relatively greater; in consequence the aerofoil is pushed up. This reduction in pressure produces double the resultant force generated by air being deflected down, i.e. two-thirds of the total lift generated. (Fig.5)

Resultant

Fig.5

Airflow →

— Pressure
+ Distribution

Whereas cambered aerofoils are usually of rigid construction, this does not apply to the powered parachute. This type of aeroplane does not use the round type of canopy with which some people are familiar. It uses a **ram-air** type of canopy composed of a number of individual cells linked to each other by vents. This allows a rapid and uniform inflation when the open front of the canopy is faced into wind or moves forward into the airflow. When inflated, an aerofoil section is formed which generates lift enabling the machine to glide and fly like a conventional aeroplane. (Fig.5A)

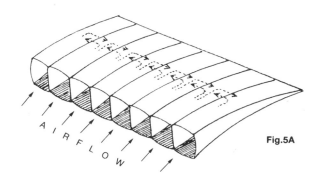

AIRFLOW

Fig.5A

11

Prove the effect of camber for yourself. Take a piece of thick paper or thin card and blow onto it so that your breath hits the top of the leading edge. You will see the card rise in the airflow caused by your breath. (Fig.6)

Fig.6

Forces at Play

In beginning to talk about forces it is worth spending a moment or two gaining an understanding as to what takes place when a force is applied or created.

An object rests at point A and on moving it along in direction B one can say that a 'Force' provided the movement. (Fig.7)

A ———— Force ———► B

Fig.7

The same can be said if the object is moved in the Direction C. (Fig.8)

C

F
O
R
C
E

Fig. 8

A

Simultaneously exert forces B and C from A, vertically and horizontally, and the object will move to D like an arrow from a bow at an angle of 45 degrees. (Fig.9)

Now think of the above diagram as a parallelogram – a shape where opposite sides and angles are equal to one another.

The diagonal A to D is the total force produced; but the object can be said to have moved part horizontally and part vertically in arriving at D.

Thus the force towards D can be said to have two components – one horizontal (A to B) and the other, vertical (A to C).

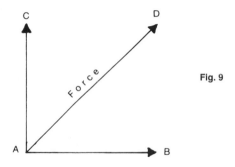

Fig. 9

These two forces are represented by the sides of the parallelogram projecting from the start of the diagonal at A. (Fig.10)

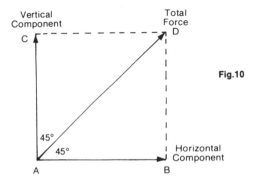

Fig.10

As the angle of the diagonal is the same between each side, the length of AB is the same as AC. In other words, the horizontal force and the vertical force are equal. Prove this by measuring them for yourself.

But what if the diagonal varies in angle? The picture may be thus. (Fig.11)

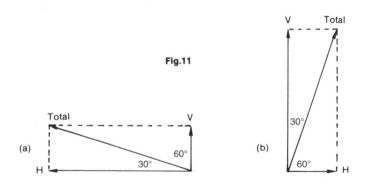

Fig.11

13

In (a) above the horizontal component H is three times as much as the vertical one V.

In (b) the opposite is the case.

You can now see that given a resultant force (a diagonal) it is possible to establish the value of its components by measurement alone – unless you are a trigonometry addict!

Once again, try it for yourself. (Fig.12)

Fig. 12

The principle we have just discussed is known as the **Parallelogram of Forces**.

No apologies are offered for this slight incursion into mathematics because in grasping same you will be well equipped to understand the forces at play in flight.

The Four Forces in Flight

There are four main forces at play when an aeroplane flies.

WEIGHT – Acts vertically down (gravity) and has to be overcome by a force acting vertically upwards so that flight may be sustained.

It is basically constant in flight except for a decrease taking place with the usage of fuel.

LIFT – Acts upwards to overcome weight. It will vary according to airspeed and/or angle of attack. It acts at right angles to the airflow but not necessarily in exact opposition to weight when out of level flight as you will see later.

THRUST – Produces the forward movement to provide an airflow over the wing.

It will vary according to the power applied and/or the angle of attack.

DRAG – The force which tends to hold back or resist forward movement.

It will vary with airspeed and angle of attack and acts in opposition to thrust.

The four forces are depicted in Fig.13

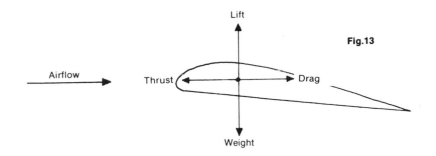

Fig.13

Equilibrium

An aircraft maintaining constant height at a constant speed will have Lift exactly equal to Weight (no climb or descent) and Thrust will be exactly equal to Drag (no acceleration or deceleration).
In this state the aircraft is said to be in **equilibrium**.

Drag

Drag needs some amplification as it comes in two distinct types.

Induced Drag

The first type is directly linked with the production of lift.
We talked earlier about the angle of attack at which the aerofoil meets the airflow and how this deflected the airflow downwards.
The resultant upwards force, acting at right angles to this downward flow, is 'bent' back out of the vertical and at once produces two components.
The vertical one we already know to be lift. The horizontal one acts rearwards and is naturally a drag component. It is known as **Induced Drag**. (Fig.14)

Fig.14

It is now appropriate to look at what is happening on the creation of induced drag.
The unequal pressure distribution, which enables a wing to produce lift

also produces this drag. The increased pressure below the wing tries to equalise with the decreased pressure on the top surface and it does so at the wing tips. (Fig.15)

Fig.15

This movement results in a two directional flow of air – outwards underneath the wing and inwards over the top. The shift in direction is most pronounced towards the tips. (Fig.16)

Inwards over top   AIRFLOW   Outwards over bottom

Fig.16

When the two airstreams meet there is a cross flow situation which results in the formation of a spiral flow known as a trailing edge vortex.

The numerous trailing edge vortices so formed end up moving towards each tip to create two main wing tip vortices. (Fig.17)

Fig. 17

Any disturbance to the smooth flow of air will naturally cause drag. In this case it cannot be avoided as where lift is produced so is induced drag.

Attempts are made to reduce the vortex effect by the use of wings of long span related to a narrow chord – usually associated with sailplanes.

Side-tracking drag for a moment, you may as well know of the term used for describing the relationship of span to chord.

It is called **Aspect Ratio** and is a figure derived from dividing the span by the chord.

See how wings of similar area can have entirely different aspect ratios. (Fig.18)

$$A/R = \frac{20}{5} = 4$$

$$A/R = \frac{50}{2} = 25$$

Fig.18

Wings of low aspect ratio are usually associated with fighter or aerobatic aircraft where rapid manoeuvrability is the order of the day but plenty of power is available to deal with the induced drag.

High aspect ratio wings are very much confined to sailplanes where minimum drag is critical in the absence of power and the need for minimum sink and maximum penetration count for everything.

Form Drag

The second type of drag is caused by the aircraft itself. Any object moving through air or water will experience a resistance to such movement.

Walking against a wind is an example you must be used to. Do this with a fully opened umbrella in front of you and you will be left with no doubt.

The same effect is experienced by an aircraft as it is propelled through the air. This resistance is known as **Form Drag** and it is reduced as far as possible by streamlining. (Fig.19)

Fig.19

To those who may think that the open front of a powered parachute canopy is likely to cause considerable drag, in actual fact there is a **back pressure** created by the air in the inflated wing which produces an invisible leading edge. (Fig.19A)

BACK
PRESSURE   **Fig.19A**

Form Drag is also known by the term **Profile Drag**.

17

Speed Squared Law

For those mathematically inclined Form Drag is proportional to the square of the speed.

You may have noticed that when increasing speed on a bicycle the resistance (drag) becomes so much greater than you expected.

The reason is that when you double your speed the drag created is **four** times as much. Treble your speed and drag is **nine** times more; ten times the speed and drag is **one hundred** times greater.

This 'Pearl of Wisdom' is known as the **Speed Squared Law**.

Now this law applies equally to lift as it does to drag. In other words, if you double the speed you produce four times the lift – and so on.

Varying the Angle of Attack

The angle of attack is the angle at which the wing meets the **Airflow** and it can vary according to the way you fly your aircraft.

As the angle of attack is increased so is the speed of the airflow over the top. At the same time a decrease of speed occurs on the underside of the wing. The pressure difference between top and bottom discussed earlier is thus widened and the upward force is increased.

However, as the angle increases the resultant force produced is 'leaning' further back with only a partial increase in the lift component but a substantial increase of induced drag. (Fig.20)

Fig.20

As long as there is sufficient power to maintain the same airspeed, increasing the angle of attack will produce more lift but only up to a point. More on this later.

Climb too steeply with insufficient power to cope and although your wing may be pointing upwards, as you slow down the aircraft will just 'mush' and the actual flight path will be nearly horizontal as it can climb no more. (Fig.21)

This configuration is suitable for the situation where you wish to fly slowly without loss of height. However it can be a critical position to put yourself in and why this can be so will be made clear when 'stalling' is discussed shortly.

Fig.21

Direction
Pointed

Airflow

Direction
of Travel

Alternatively, you feel you are descending too fast and without applying any extra power you climb in order to slow down. Once again if the power is insufficient to take you along your chosen flight path the aircraft will 'mush' and the flight path will be different from the direction in which the wing is pointing. (Fig.22)

Direction
Pointed

Direction
of Travel

Airflow

Fig.22

Remember, the angle of attack is the angle at which the wing meets the airflow and not the direction in which it is pointing. Once the angle reaches a critical point and that point is exceeded then lift breaks down.

The Stall

For the aerofoil to produce lift efficiently the flow of air over its surface must be smooth and unbroken. Being endowed with the properties of a fluid there is a tendency for the particles of air to stick to the aerofoil. However, there is a breaking point. (Fig.23)

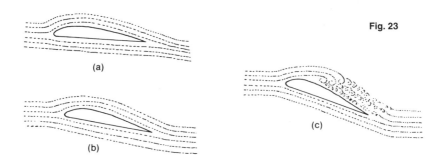

Fig. 23

(a)

(b)

(c)

Situations (a) and (b) show the aerofoil at different angles of attack with the airflow behaving as it should do.

However, in situation (c) the angle has become too steep for the air to cling to the upper surface any longer and it breaks away thus destroying the smooth flow and the reduction in pressure which provides the major part of total lift.

In short, the wing is said to have **Stalled** and the airspeed at which this occurs is known as the **Stalling Speed**. If your airspeed is allowed to drop too low your angle of attack will become too high and two-thirds of the total lift will go at the stall. The angle at which this occurs is around 15°.

The behaviour of an aircraft in a stall will vary according to the type of aircraft. Broadly speaking the pattern is this. At the point of stall the nose will drop and as the aircraft takes up the nose down attitude the airspeed will begin to build up. On reaching flying speed normal flight can be resumed.

The stalling speed for a given aeroplane may be set at a certain figure. However, the same aeroplane can be made heavier or lighter according to the amount of fuel/passengers carried.

If heavier, an above normal airspeed will be needed to produce the extra lift required. If lighter, the less lift required means flight can be maintained at below normal airspeed so the stalling speed can vary.

Another point you must watch. Where the stalling speed is greater, the longer will be your take-off or landing run.

Safe airspeed is one of the most vital things to watch in flight. Maintaining sufficient airspeed keeps the angle of attack below the stalling angle.

'Thrust' with no Power

The question might be running through your mind as to where an aircraft with no engine can obtain 'thrust' in order to produce airspeed. The answer is best given with a simple analogy first and a technical explanation afterwards.

A railway truck standing on a level track will not move forward until an engine comes along to push or pull it. However, place the truck on a sloping track and on releasing the brake it will roll downhill unaided.

So it is with an aircraft with no engine (or engine off). It uses gravity to provide thrust. Also by adopting a nose down attitude lift now acts forwards as well as upwards. This combined with weight produces a forward force or hypothetical 'Thrust'. (Fig.24a). At the same time it can be seen how in this attitude drag contributes to produce a resultant upwards force opposite to weight which is greater than lift. (Fig.24b)

Lift/Drag Ratio

At a given airspeed and angle of attack a wing will produce a certain amount of lift together with a certain amount of drag.

The relationship between the two is called the **Lift/Drag Ratio**.

Fig. 24

If the lift generated happens to be 10 times the drag then the Lift/Drag Ratio is said to be 10/1.

Every aeroplane has an airspeed at which the angle of attack will produce the maximum amount of lift for the minimum amount of drag.

Knowing that particular airspeed is crucial should you ever find yourself with no engine and the need to reach a safe landing ground some way ahead. It is at this airspeed that you will cover the maximum distance before arriving on 'Mother Earth'.

Reducing airspeed with the idea of staying up longer to cover a greater distance is not on. The increased angle of attack this brings about may increase lift and thus a reduced rate of sink; but, there will also be an increase in drag which will reduce the Lift/Drag Ratio and so reduce the distance you can cover in the time remaining in the air.

Increasing airspeed to arrive there before running out of height will also not work. The increase in airspeed requires a decrease in angle of attack which also brings about a decrease in lift. Although drag reduces as well, the amount is not enough to prevent yet again, a reduced Lift/Drag Ratio. Examples of the three situations can be seen in Fig.25.

Fig. 25

Best Gliding Angle

You will no doubt eventually come across the term 'best gliding angle' – again expressed as a ratio, say 10/1. This is only another way of saying that the aeroplane will travel 10 feet forward for every 1 foot of height lost.

Flying at the best gliding angle assumes you will be flying at the best airspeed – that which provides the maximum L/D ratio.

For the glide angle to be at its best in practical terms presupposes you are flying in still air. Given a headwind the angle in relation to the ground will be steeper; with a tail wind it becomes more shallow.

Whilst mathematically difficult to demonstrate, you can increase speed in a headwind and decrease same in a tailwind to achieve maximum distance.

This is because an increase in speed in a headwind means steepening the glide and therefore moving out of the stronger wind aloft compared with that nearer the ground.

Conversely, easing off speed in a tailwind means a more shallow glide and therefore more time in that stronger wind aloft to attain more distance.

Best Rate of climb and Best Angle of Climb

The handling instructions for many aeroplanes give two climbing speeds for the aeroplane concerned.

– Best Rate of Climb

– Best Angle of Climb

There is a difference between the two though you may be forgiven if at first you think this is not so.

Best rate of climb refers to attaining the maximum amount of height in the minimum amount of time at maximum power. The manual will give you an airspeed at which to fly to achieve this rate.

Now it may be that the angle of climb that this rate involves is insufficient to clear an obstruction on your take-off path.

To cater for such a situation the manual gives you an alternative airspeed at which to fly. This airspeed will be lower than for 'Best Rate' but the angle of climb will be greater.

By flying more slowly it takes longer to reach the obstruction but in the extra time bought enough height is reached to clear it even though the rate of climb itself is reduced.

Using hypothetical figures the situation is depicted in Fig.26.

Fig. 26

1000' in 1¼ mins   1000' in 1 min

Best Angle of Climb 850' p.min at 40 mph

Best Rate of Climb 1000' p.min at 50 mph

If you are really keen, measure it for yourself. On the other hand you would do better listening to guidance from your instructor on obstruction clearance rather than becoming immersed in theory.

On no account in normal circumstances should you be taking off from any site with an obstruction that warrants the above assessment. If you are forced to land in such a place it would be better to dismantle the aeroplane rather than take off and dismantle yourself.

Varying the Angle of Attack can be summed up thus.

- A decrease in the angle reduces lift, increases speed and thereby increases drag.
- An increase in the angle increases lift, decreases speed and . . .

Why the hesitation you may ask? The reason is this; the decrease in speed will naturally bring about a decrease in **Form** (or profile) Drag but at the same time the increased angle of attack sees an increase in **Induced** Drag.

Remember, Induced Drag is at its greatest at low speeds. Therefore the vortex effect is also at a maximum at low speeds.

The wake turbulence from vortex effect is thus going to be at its greatest during take-off and landing when angles of attack are high and speed is relatively low.

Wake turbulence is covered in the section on 'Meteorology' as it is very much influenced by atmospheric conditions.

Finally, increase the angle of attack too much and you will stall.

The Next Step

By now you should be gaining a good working knowledge as to **why** your aircraft can fly – and more importantly, when it will cease to do so if you do not watch your airspeed.

Most of what has been discussed so far has assumed the aircraft to be in straight and level flight. In reality a journey from one place to another is going to necessitate plenty of departures from the straight and level. These departures can be brought about by intention or very often by turbulent air.

Taking first the case of turbulent air we are talking about those occasions when the aircraft can be dislodged or turned about in relation to its flight path by the air itself. The answer to this flight condition lies in the stability built into the aircraft.

Stability

Stability is a condition which enables an aircraft to revert to its normal flight path without pilot input on those occasions when it is deflected from same.

To understand this means examining the different axes about which an aircraft can move. (Fig.26)

We will now look at the way in which stability is built in to cope with movements about each of the axes shown above.

Fig. 27

AXIS	Longitudinal	Vertical	Lateral
PLANE	Rolling	Yawing	Pitching
MANOEUVRE	Banking	Change of Direction or Heading	Nose Up Nose Down
CONTROL	Lateral	Directional	Longitudinal

Dihedral

Obtaining a stability in the **Rolling Plane** is achieved by **Dihedral**. Looking at most aircraft head-on you will see that the tips of the wings are invariably higher than the roots. The angle thus subtended is known as the angle of dihedral. (Fig.28)

Fig. 28

Angle of Dihedral

(a)

In turbulent air a wing may drop.

(b)

As the wing drops it will tend to slip in the direction of the drop. This creates a 'crosswind' component in the airflow in relation to the wing. (Fig.29)

Fig.29

As the airflow meets the wing in this situation the lower wing meets the airflow at a greater angle of attack than the upper one and so provides increased lift moving the wing back into level flight again. (Fig.30)

Fig.30

Stability in the Yawing Plane and Pitching Plane is normally obtained by fixed surfaces placed to the rear of the C. of G. although there are occasions when they will be found to the front of this point.

The surface acting in the yawing plane is called a **Fin** or **Keel**; the one acting in the pitching plane is known as a **Tailplane**. (Fig.31)

Fin

Tailplane

Fig.31

Keel

When the aircraft is dislodged from its intended flight path these fixed surfaces are presented to the airflow. The air is deflected and a force is set up at right angles to the deflected air. This force moves the aircraft back into its original path. (Fig.32)

Fig.32

Some microlights do not have a tailplane as such. With these types of aircraft there is usually a marked degree of **Sweepback** on the wings. It is the area in proximity to each wing tip that acts as the fixed surface required aft of the C. of G. to give stability in the pitching plane. (Fig.33)

25

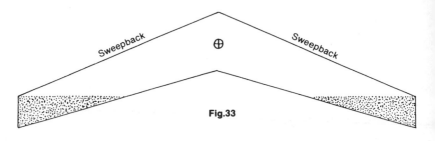

Fig.33

Others solve the pitch stability problem in trailing edges which are 'reflexed' so that in a dive the effect is to endeavour to restore level flight. This reflex is usually to be found on the inboard halves of the wing. (Fig.34)

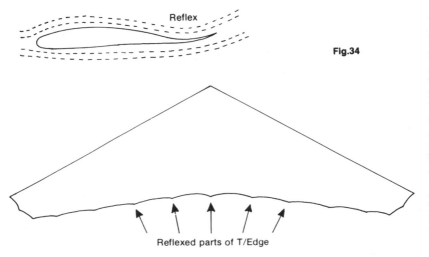

Reflex

Fig.34

Reflexed parts of T/Edge

Centre of Pressure

Stability can also be influenced by variations in angle of attack. For simplicity sake lift has so far been depicted as a single force line acting at right angles to the airflow.

In fact that single line represents the total lift generated which varies over the whole surface of the wing. (Fig.35)

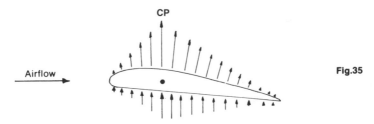

CP

Airflow

Fig.35

The point on the aerofoil at which all the lift is said to act is known as the **Centre of Pressure** and it varies with the angle of attack.

An increase in this angle will see the centre of pressure (CP) move forward; a decrease will see it move aft. (Fig.36)

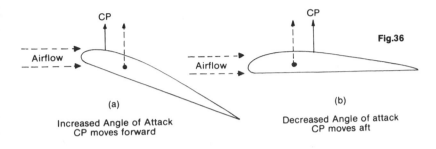

CP

CP

Airflow

Airflow

Fig.36

(a)

Increased Angle of Attack
CP moves forward

(b)

Decreased Angle of attack
CP moves aft

Now look at what this can do to stability. (Fig.37)

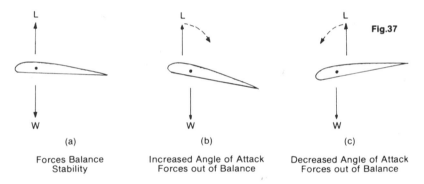

L

L

L

Fig.37

W

W

W

(a)

Forces Balance
Stability

(b)

Increased Angle of Attack
Forces out of Balance

(c)

Decreased Angle of Attack
Forces out of Balance

So, apart from built-in stability being needed to combat turbulence, it is also needed to compensate for any movement of centre of pressure.

A particular contribution to this stability is the tailplane on a fixed wing (three-axis) machine and the reflexed trailing edge on others.

Manoeuvring

Here we are going to be concerned with the intentional movement out of a flight path – the business of going where we want to when we want to.

This may be a climb, descent, change of heading or maybe a combination of two at once – such as a climbing or a descending turn.

Under principles of flight we are not really concerned with **how** to manoeuvre – that is the job of the flying instructor. The aim at this stage is to become familiar with the control surfaces that produce manoeuvres and the effect each has in doing so.

Stability was achieved by **fixed** surfaces which when presented to the airflow caused the aircraft to return to its original flight path. It will therefore come as no surprise to know that manoeuvring is achieved by **movable** surfaces (in most cases) which are introduced into the airflow to set up forces that will cause a change of flight path.

Such control is known as aerodynamic but this form does not apply to **flexwing** types of aeroplane – easily recognised by their hang glider format of wing.

These machines, commonly known as 'trikes', do not have movable control surfaces in the traditional sense about to be described. It will be seen later that a trike manoeuvres by a principle known as **weight shift**.

So now on to the manoeuvres themselves by aerodynamic control.

Change of Direction or Heading

If you were to think in the context of a boat you could be forgiven for thinking that the above section title would be better reduced to one word – turning.

In flying however, a turn is a combination of two manoeuvres – change of direction and bank. For the moment we will consider one at a time to avoid complication.

Change of direction is usually associated with the use of **rudder**. Very few people will not be familiar with this term if only in relation, again, to boats.

A rudder will normally be a moveable surface attached to the fin. (Fig.38).

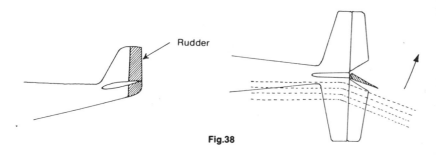

Fig.38

In Fig.38 you can see that as the rudder is deployed into the airflow, it deflects the air to one side thus setting up a force in the opposite direction causing the aeroplane to rotate about its vertical axis.

Changing direction in a powered parachute is effected by depressing the left or right trailing edge of the canopy. This is achieved by means of toggles to which lines are attached reaching out to the trailing edge extremities of the canopy. As one toggle is pulled, the relevant trailing edge of the canopy is depressed and the drag thus produced results in a change of direction. (Fig.38A)

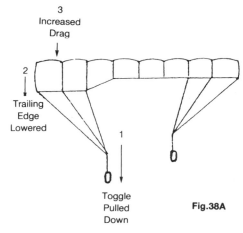

Fig.38A

Some microlights are not fitted with a rudder but have moving surfaces at the extremities of the wings known as **Tip Draggers**. These tip draggers operate independently of each other and their effect is best depicted by an analogy to water.

If you are under way in a rowing boat with the oars shipped, place one oar in the water and very quickly the boat will turn in the direction of the immersed oar. The oar has caused drag and the boat has pivoted about that drag point. (Fig.39)

Fig.39

Whichever means are used – rudder, canopy adjustment or draggers – the change of direction about the vertical axis is known as **Yaw** and a secondary or further effect occurs. (Fig.40)

With two unequal lift forces the wing outboard of the turn will rise and the inboard wing will drop producing a rolling movement as a further effect of yaw.

This rolling movement can be increased by dihedral. An aircraft is not like a car which follows the way it is headed due to wheel contact with solid ground. As it changes direction in a yaw, although it will take up a new

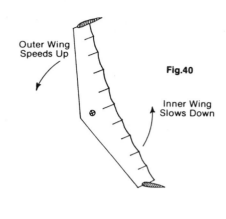

Fig.40

Outer Wing Speeds Up

Inner Wing Slows Down

(a) Left rudder applied
or Left dragger applied.
Forces set up at tip.

(b) Wing pivots about deployed dragger.
Aircraft yaws to left.
Lift increases on outer wing as it speeds up.
Lift decreases on inner wing as it slows down.
Rolling movement is set up.

Heading, for a short time it will 'skid' in the direction of its original flight path. This affects the direction of the airflow in relation to the wing. (Fig.41)

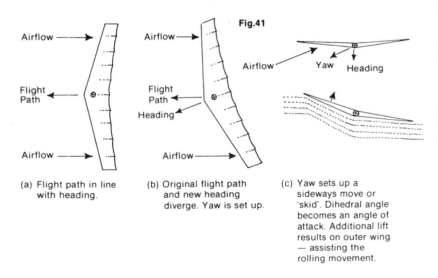

Fig.41

(a) Flight path in line
with heading.

(b) Original flight path
and new heading
diverge. Yaw is set up.

(c) Yaw sets up a
sideways move or
'skid'. Dihedral angle
becomes an angle of
attack. Additional lift
results on outer wing
— assisting the
rolling movement.

The flexwing or trike has no rudder, draggers or canopy adjustment facility so how does it change direction? It does so by the further effect of banking – the manoeuvre we discuss next.

Banking

Banking is manoeuvring the aircraft in the rolling plane.

You have already seen how this can come about as a further effect of yawing; in fact this is the way in which a 2-axis aeroplane banks when equipped with only a rudder and no ailerons. We will now be looking at the controls that cause banking as a direct result.

Ailerons

The conventional form of control used in banking is exercised through the medium of ailerons – moveable surfaces set in the trailing edge at the end of each wing. When activated, one goes up and the other goes down thus setting up a movement in the rolling plane. (Fig.42)

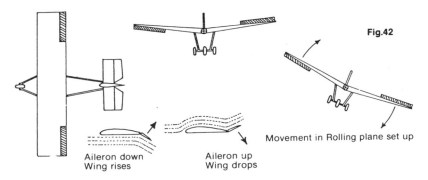

Fig.42

Movement in Rolling plane set up

Aileron down
Wing rises

Aileron up
Wing drops

Ailerons are of particular use for their ability to keep a wing down when taxying, taking off or landing in cross winds. This can be most helpful in the case of some microlights.

There is a secondary effect induced by banking. As the bank occurs the aircraft will sideslip towards the lower wing. This effectively sets up a sideways component in the direction at which the airflow is met. This makes the aircraft want to 'weathercock' into the airflow resulting in a turn as it does so. (Fig.43)

Co-ordination of rudder and aileron by inducing skid to counteract slip produces a balanced turn and is an art to which you must devote practice.

The use of ailerons can bring about another interesting effect.

The aileron on the outer wing being in the down position alters the shape of the aerofoil and effects an **increase** in angle of attack. The other aileron going up does the opposite on the lower wing – it **decreases** the angle.

You may say why bother as the two will cancel each other out – in practice this is broadly speaking the case. However, the increased angle of attack brought about by the downgoing aileron can produce sufficient

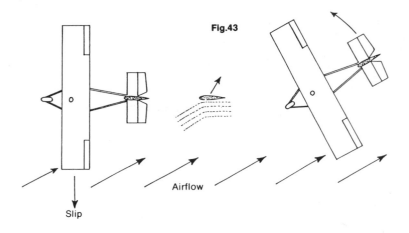

Fig.43

Airflow

Slip

extra induced drag to force the aircraft to yaw in the opposite direction to the bank.

This effect is known as **Adverse Yaw** and it can be reduced by the fitting of **Differential Ailerons**. Here the arc of the downgoing aileron is restricted to a much smaller one compared with the arc of the upgoing one thus ensuring that the drag on the lower wing will always be greater than that on the upper wing. (Fig.44)

Fig. 44

Spoilers

Another form of control for banking, particularly for microlights, is that of spoiler effect.

Spoilers are movable surfaces on the top of the wings placed at the point of maximum lift so that when presented to the airflow they disrupt lift in the immediate vicinity. (Fig.45) When activated independently of each other, with unequal lift produced, a rolling movement takes place. However, drag is also playing a part in this situation and the activated spoiler will have a similar effect to that of a dragger (or one oar in the water). The lower wing will slow down thus inducing yaw. In other words, when you bank using a spoiler you also initiate a turn as a further effect.

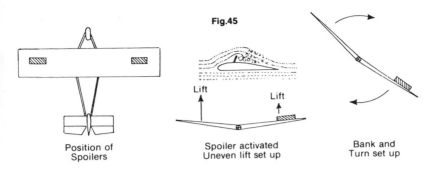

Fig.45

Position of
Spoilers

Spoiler activated
Uneven lift set up

Bank and
Turn set up

Spoilers, when used independently of each other for banking, are known as **Spoilerons**.

Weight Shift

Earlier it was said that the flexwing or trike type manoeuvred by the principle of weight shift. Now this principle when applied to the trike is actually by further effect – a point worthy of some explanation prior to discussing it in the context of banking.

With a trike, such weight as can be 'shifted' consists of the pilot/trike unit itself. However, being suspended from a single focal point beneath the wing, the natural tendency is for this combination to behave as a pendulum.

Now the only way to dislodge this pendulum (or weight) from equilibrium, when you are part and parcel of it, is to push or pull against another part of the structure not integral with the pilot/trike unit. In this case it will be the 'A' frame which is rigidly attached to the wing.

But on the ground pushing or pulling on the control bar, which is the base of the 'A' frame, will readily move the wing in any direction be it side to side or up and down. Far from being the rigid structure against which to obtain an opposite force you may think.

However, in flight the situation is very different. The inherent stability of the wing moving through the air makes it reluctant to move out of the stable state and thus it becomes sufficiently 'solid' for the purpose in mind. (Fig.46)

So, when airborne, pushing or pulling on the bar (or moving it to one side or the other) will in the immediate instant move the wing only slightly but it will move the pendular pilot/trike unit out of equilibrium.

In other words it enables the weight (or centre of gravity) to be moved at will and the moment this happens the wing will now move in the direction the weight has shifted or rotate against the direction in which the weight has shifted – whichever way you want to look at it.

On Ground   Fig.46   In Flight

Thus, bank is set up in a trike by moving the bar **away** from the intended direction of bank; the weight moves in the opposite direction and the wing banks in the desired direction. (Fig.47)

Fig.47

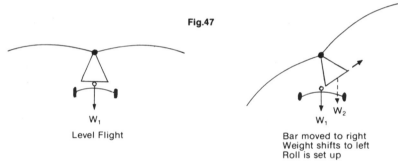

Level Flight

Bar moved to right
Weight shifts to left
Roll is set up

There are two other factors which assist in effecting roll in some flexwing types.

Billow Shift

The first factor is a flexibility built into the sail which 'gives' in the sense that any re-distribution of loading induced by weight shift (or draggers in the case of an Eagle type microlight) allows a change of wing format to take place.

Without delving too deeply into the mechanics, the process is known as **Billow Shift** and it works this way.

– Bank is initiated by weight shift (or dragger) in the direction of intended bank.

– The flexibility in the wing induces slackness in the trailing edge of the banked wing and a tightening in that of the other wing.

- The slackness allows increased billow in the banked wing – the trailing edge rises and the angle of attack is **decreased**.
- The tightening on the other wing pulls the trailing edge down thus **increasing** the angle of attack.
- The result is less lift in the banked wing and more lift on the outer wing – thus setting up a rolling movement. (Fig.48)

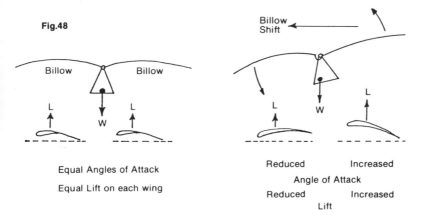

Fig.48

Billow Shift

Billow   Billow

L   L
W

Equal Angles of Attack

Equal Lift on each wing

Reduced   Increased

Angle of Attack

Reduced   Increased

Lift

As an aside, billow shift also serves another useful purpose. In rough weather any strong gust striking one wing will induce the slackness in that wing and the excess air is spilled out thus reducing the effect of the turbulence.

Roach

The second factor referred to in assisting roll is really an extension of the billow shift process except the movement of the wing is confined more to the tips.

The factor is known as **Roach** and the effect is similar to that of ailerons. (Fig.49)

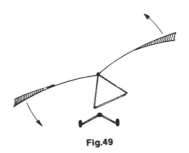

Fig.49

Nose Up/Nose Down

Manoeuvring nose up and nose down is primarily related to raising or lowering the angle of attack and thereby controlling airspeed.

The movement is known as **Pitching**.

Contrary to popular belief, unlike a car where speed is controlled by power, it is pitch control that governs airspeed in flight except on take-off and at touch down.

Pitch down and you will increase airspeed; pitch up and your airspeed will drop away.

Power is used to determine climb and descent. Increase power to climb; reduce power to descend.

But back to the manoeuvre itself. Pitching takes place about the lateral axis of the aeroplane.

Again, such control can be aerodynamic (movable surfaces) or by weight shift.

Elevators

Aerodynamic control is in the form of movable surfaces called **Elevators** attached to the tailplane or any other fixed surface used to obtain stability in the pitching plane. (Fig.50)

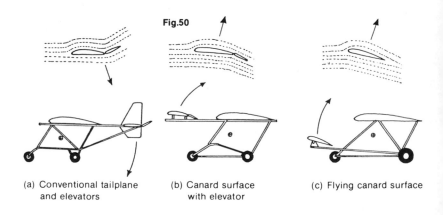

Fig.50

(a) Conventional tailplane and elevators

(b) Canard surface with elevator

(c) Flying canard surface

The configuration in (b) is worth some elaboration. The canard in this situation is a form of additional lifting surface, a 'mini' wing out front for the want of a better description.

This canard wing is set at a slightly higher angle of attack than the main wing. As the aircraft approaches a stall the canard therefore stalls first, the nose drops thus preventing the main wing reaching the stall point in anything but induced abnormal flight.

This arrangement produces a very forgiving form of aircraft. It is not used as widely as it might be due to the increased form drag produced.

Weight Shift

In the case of a flexwing aeroplane the bar is used to displace weight culminating in a change of angle of attack. (Fig.51)

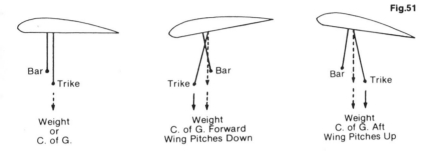

Fig.51

Bar
Trike
Weight
or
C. of G.

Bar
Trike
Weight
C. of G. Forward
Wing Pitches Down

Bar
Trike
Weight
C. of G. Aft
Wing Pitches Up

Alternative methods of pitch control by weight shift are these.

The pilot in some cases sits on a seat which is freely suspended below the wing. Weight is here re-distributed by pulling or pushing on the structure around the pilot.

Sometimes the seat is connected by cables to movable control surfaces which move to assist the input required by the shift of weight.

Examples are to be found in the early Quicksilver type aircraft where a sideways movement of the suspended pilot also activates a rudder. Again, the Eagle type seat is connected to an elevator on the canard foreplane.

There is also the method where the seating position is rigid but the pilot has the latitude to move backwards and forwards within sufficient limits to exercise full pitch control such as on Pterodactyl type aircraft. (Fig.52)

W
Weight
Position

Fig.52

Shift
W   W
New   Original
Weight Weight

Diagrammatically the position of the four forces in pitching by weight shift is shown below. (Fig.53)

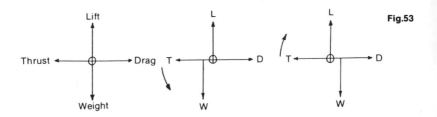

Fig.53

Pitch can also be affected by the thrust line of the engine in that there may be a change of trim in certain aircraft as power is increased or decreased. Such changes will have to be anticipated quickly particularly when in close proximity to the ground.

The forces at play are shown in Fig.54

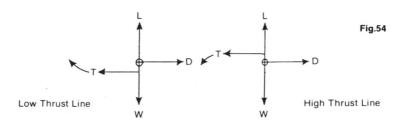

Fig.54

Pitch control in powered parachutes departs from the norm in the absence of elevators or the ability to move the wing as a total entity.

In fact the normal control is by power alone. An increase in power increases airspeed which in turn increases lift and the machine climbs. Reduce power and the reverse happens. Again, in the absence of aero-dynamic pitch control or a movable wing, you must understand that you cannot apply power, ease the stick forward or pull the bar back and thus increase airspeed. You may now have deduced that the powered parachute is inevitably a fixed speed aeroplane in level flight; any adjustment of power in this configuration will result in a climb or a descent.

There is an element of pitch control which can be exercised when both toggles are pulled down together. The depressed trailing edges on both sides of the canopy cause an increased angle of attack which momentarily increases both lift and drag. The lift reduces the rate of descent and the drag reduces the speed so application of this control input can be a useful contribution to making a precise flare at the point of touch-down.

Before leaving pitch control it is important to know that the position of the centre of gravity (CG) has an influence. Too far to the rear and the aeroplane can become unstable in pitch. On flexwing aeroplanes operating by weight shift there can be alternative hang points to which the trike unit can be attached. This is to allow the pilot to vary the trim speed – or hands off speed as it is normally called. Be careful in selecting a point too far rearwards as this in effect is moving the CG the same way thus leading to instability.

High Speed Stall

One final word on pitch control. You will remember that when yaw was set up there was a moment when the aircraft was heading in the new direction but actually travelling along the original path.

The same sort of situation can arise in the use of pitch control but with much more dire effect if you have insufficient height.

You are diving at a fairly high speed and suddenly decide to pitch the nose up. The nose will certainly go up but for a time the aircraft will continue on its downward path resulting in a sharp increase in the angle of attack.

If the stalling angle is exceeded then the smooth airflow over the wing will break away and a stall will take place even though your airspeed may be well above stalling speed as you know it.

You will have been subjected to what is known as a **High Speed Stall** and this condition is far from clever close to the ground. However, with the low wing loading normally associated with microlights there should not be a problem with this type of aeroplane.

Manoeuvres out of Straight and Level

So far the effect of controls has been discussed taking each control in isolation and assuming application is being made from the stable state of straight and level flight.

What if the same inputs are made when out of straight and level?

The situation is best grasped by understanding that in whatever attitude your aeroplane finds itself, the input of a particular control will have the same effect on it as in level flight.

That is, the movement will still be in relation to the appropriate axis of the aeroplane. However, the movement might be far from the same in relation to the horizon or the ground.

The effect is best shown visually. (Fig.55)

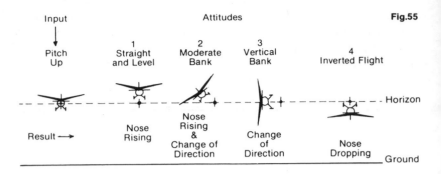

Notice how in attitude 2 the use of pitch up has not only raised the nose but has caused a change in direction. In attitude 3 it is acting totally as a rudder whilst in 4 the outcome is the nose dropping.

Take a small model of an aeroplane and demonstrate to yourself the movements it should make as you apply imaginary control inputs of not only pitch but yaw and roll also – all with the model in various attitudes.

Turning

The most frequent manoeuvre you will make is a turn. Earlier it was said that in flying it needed a blend of two manoeuvres at the same time to execute a turn – a combination of roll and yaw. In fact pitch plays a part as well.

You have already learned that the input of yaw on its own results in a change of heading with the aeroplane itself tending to skid along its original path – fly off at a tangent you might say.

Inducing your machine to prescribe a circle needs the input of a force acting towards the centre of that circle – as if the aeroplane is tethered to a pole and forced to fly round it.

The force used to do just this is lift. As roll is induced and the wing is banked – note the disposition of the forces in the resulting parallelogram of forces. (Fig.56)

You can see how lift divides into two other forces – one acting vertically and the other an inwards force pulling the aeroplane towards the centre of the turn. This force is known as **Centripetal Force** (CP) forget for a moment the fact that V is now less than L – more on this later.

However, induce roll on its own and the ensuing slip will cause a loss in height.

An input of just the right amount of yaw sorts this out as the resulting skid counteracts the slip – demonstrating the simultaneous combination of roll and yaw needed to initiate a balanced turn.

As the turn develops, the rudder will begin to act as an elevator due to the attitude of the aeroplane and once again height could be lost; also the outer wing travels faster than the inner one in a turn so the increased lift on the outer wing could induce more roll than required.

Both these possibilities are checked by an input of pitch-up control at the same time taking off yaw and any tendency towards too much roll is countered by easing of roll input. (Fig.57)

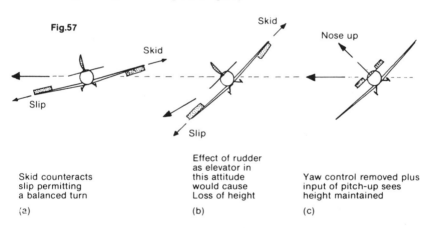

Fig.57

Skid counteracts
slip permitting
a balanced turn

(a)

Effect of rudder
as elevator in
this attitude
would cause
Loss of height

(b)

Yaw control removed plus
input of pitch-up sees
height maintained

(c)

To achieve a very tight turn – one of small radius – means increasing bank so that centripetal force (CP) is increased in order to achieve this aim. (Fig.58)

Fig.58

However, increasing CP results in a further decrease in force V which acts vertically to support weight (**W**). Again, the problem this can cause and the avoidance of same will be discussed later.

The Trike in a Turn

The question must be going through your mind as to where the 'Trike' figures in all this. After all there is no rudder or draggers to provide that initial yaw to balance the turn.

In fact the trike cannot yaw in the conventional sense but in turning overall it does have other facets which play a part.

Turning a trike starts with inducing bank and setting up centripetal force in the same way as just discussed. As bank occurs, slip results and the situation is thus. (Fig.59)

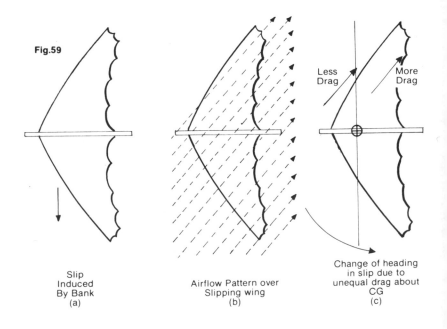

Fig.59

Less Drag   More Drag

Slip
Induced
By Bank
(a)

Airflow Pattern over
Slipping wing
(b)

Change of heading
in slip due to
unequal drag about
CG
(c)

In (c) above, the form drag will be greater aft of the centre of gravity (CG) due to there being more sail area in this sector. The varying drag values induce a change of heading without the need for a movable surface such as a rudder.

Also, some trikes have a vertical fin surface above or below the wing aft of the CG. (Fig.60)

As bank is induced a 'weathercock' effect assists a change of direction as the wing slips.

Fig.60

Once again the obvious loss of height that will come about by slip through roll input alone is countered with a pitch-up input by pushing out the bar.

At this point it might not be amiss to mention that pilots accustomed to a 3-axis control system – the name given to control by rudder, elevator and ailerons – may find their initial handling of a trike a most stimulating experience!

This is because the control movement with the bar will be opposite to what has probably become instinctive.

Suffice it to say, this is not the problem many think it to be. Countless pilots fly both types without thinking about it – simply because they underwent conversion tuition with a good trike instructor who was understanding of their needs.

The Balanced Turn

Finally, how can you tell if your turn is balanced? There are instruments available but if you, or just your head, is out in the open there is no need for them.

Suppose you enter a left hand turn. Too much roll input and as you slip, the airstream will strike the left hand side of your face. Too much yaw and as you skid the right hand side will feel the breeze.

You have 'got it together' when the air is striking you full in the face.

Pilots flying under cover often fix a streamer of, say, wool or ribbon outside the cockpit directly in front of them. Movement of the streamer to one side or the other will indicate slip or skid. When it is straight in line – all is well. (Fig.61)

Fig.61

Airspeed in a Turn

It is now appropriate to round off all that has been said about turning by discussing the manoeuvre in relation to air speed. This we will do from two aspects.

The Spin Off a Turn

First there is the effect from inducing yaw – carrying out a flat turn as it is called. You will recall how yaw causes a change of heading which slows down the inner wing whilst speeding up the outer one.

Now suppose your stalling speed is 30 mph and you enter a flat turn – or even unintentionally apply rudder – close to that speed. Should you do so at say 32 mph; the outer wing could well speed up to 36 mph and the inner slow down to 28 mph. At this speed the inner wing will stall and drop whilst the outer wing continues to produce lift. This can cause the aeroplane to flick over and enter a spiral descent about its vertical axis.

Similarly, if your wings are not level at the point of stall, the wing going down will meet the airflow at a greater angle of attack and stall with the other wing still producing lift.

Either way you end up in what is known as a **spin**. (Fig 62)

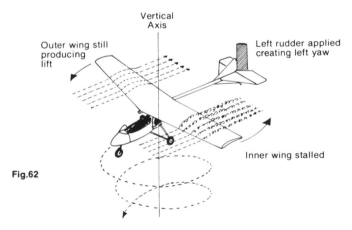

Vertical
Axis

Outer wing still
producing
lift

Left rudder applied
creating left yaw

Inner wing stalled

Fig.62

A spin must not be confused with a spiral dive. In a spin there is no increase in airspeed but vertical descent is very rapid.

In a spiral dive the aeroplane is not in a stalled condition. The nose is at a much steeper angle and the speed progressively builds up until it can reach dangerous levels.

Recovery from a spin can use up quite an amount of height which makes it a very unhealthy situation to be in low down. Modern light aeroplanes and particularly microlights are not prone to a fully developed spin; they simply start one – known as an incipient spin – and then pack in the whole idea!

Most of these aeroplanes have a facility called wash-out to reduce the change of a spin. Wash-out is a decrease in the 'angle of incidence' (a built-in angle of attack on the wing in relation to the datum line of the aeroplane) at the tips compared with that at the roots.

Thus, as a high angle of attack begins to bring on a stall, the inboard parts of the wing stall first leaving the tips still 'flying'.

However, the fact that a spin may be relatively difficult to induce in no way excuses you from maintaining the utmost vigilance over airspeed close to the stall – you could just end up proving your aeroplane is able to spin after all and find yourself 'up to your wings in aerodrome!'

Stalling Speed in a Turn

The second aspect of airspeed in the turn is rather more complicated but every effort will be made to keep the explanation as simple as possible.

Refer back to Fig.58 for a moment. As centripetal force (CP) increases in a bank, so there comes about an inevitable decrease in the vertical component (V) which supports weight (W).

If no steps are taken to counter this decrease then the result will be a descending turn.

In a bank the rate at which V drops below W is minimal at first but it becomes very marked as the bank steepens and likewise does the rate of descent.

The extent to which this happens is shown by equating V as a percentage of W in varying angles of bank. (Fig.63)

Fig.63

It should now be obvious that to execute a balanced turn with no loss of height it is crucial that V remains equal to W. this can only be achieved by increasing the angle of attack, thus increasing lift (L) and thereby increasing V until it is equal to W.

However, on increasing the angle of attack there will be an increase in induced drag and a decrease in airspeed. This calls for a gradual increase in power as the turn progresses so that adequate airspeed is maintained.

It is crucial to be aware of just what is an adequate airspeed in a turn. The question needs further examination as the stalling speed also increases in this manoeuvre.

The question by how much is a different matter if a precise explanation is to be given.

First we take a look at by how much L must be increased to ensure V equals W as bank steepens. Refer to the parallelogram of forces in Fig.64.

Fig.64

In each of the above angles of bank the value of L can be ascertained by measuring the diagonal L against the vertical side V. Without being ultra accurate (by using Pythagorus) you will see that given L = 1 in level flight then:

At 15° of bank – L required = x 1.04 ⎫
At 30° of bank – L required = x 1.16 ⎬   to keep L to equal V
At 60° of bank – L required = x 2.00 ⎭

If you have to produce twice the lift to maintain height in a turn at 60 degrees of bank then it means a substantial increase in angle of attack will be required and consequently a substantial increase in power to maintain an adequate airspeed.

It will also mean a substantial increase in your stalling speed at this angle.

Concerning the increase in stalling speed in a turn referred to earlier it will be imperceptible at first but it goes up rapidly as you steepen the bank until almost 1.5 times normal at 60° of bank. So, if your stalling speed in level flight is say 30 mph then it can be around 45 mph in a 60° banking turn.

∗ If you are interested in how this deduction is arrived at you must recall the speed squared law referred to earlier.

Lift increases at the square of the speed.

In other words, if your speed goes up by x2 then lift goes up by x4 (2x2). For the issue under discussion look at this law in reverse. If the increase in lift required is x4 then the airspeed required to produce that lift must increase by x $\sqrt{4}$ which is x 2.

So, if the minimum speed for level flight is 30 mph then to produce x 4 lift the airspeed must be 30x2 which = 60 mph.

Suppose 30 mph happens to be the stalling speed, then in this situation the stalling speed will be 60 mph.

Apply this reasoning to the examples shown above after Fig.64 – taking 30 mph as stalling speed.

Table 1

At 15° bank stalling speed increases by x $\sqrt{1.04}$ or x 1.02
At 30° bank stalling speed increases by x $\sqrt{1.16}$ or x 1.08
At 60° bank stalling speed increases by x $\sqrt{2.00}$ or x 1.41

Table 2

At 15° bank stalling speed will be 30 x 1.02 or 30.6 (31 mph)
At 30° bank stalling speed will be 30 x 1.08 or 32.4 (33 mph)
At 60° bank stalling speed will be 30 x 1.41 or 42.3 (43 mph)

Note now the increase over straight and level to 30° of bank is only +3 mph but from 30° to 60° it is most marked at another 10 mph – making 13 mph in all over level flight stalling speed.

∗∗

To sum up, it is most important that you remember this. airspeed in any form of turn be it level, climbing or descending, must be sufficient to preclude a stall; hence the need for adequate power during such manoeuvres.

Loading

Previously the tendency has been to highlight forces at play in perhaps a too one-sided way.

For example, in a bank L was shown as producing CP and V and nothing more.

Now every force must produce an equal and opposite reaction otherwise the object being acted upon would be constantly on the move and never achieve a balanced state.

In Fig. 65 you can see how W is the force that stops V continuing to take the aeroplane upwards.

47

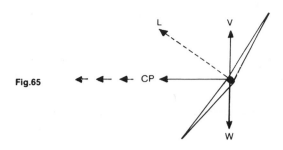

Fig.65

So, in a balanced turn there is a force acting outwards to balance centripetal force (CP) and this is called **Centrifugal Reaction** (CR) – known by some perhaps wrongly as centrifugal force. Anyway, we will talk about it as a force where it suits. (Fig.66)

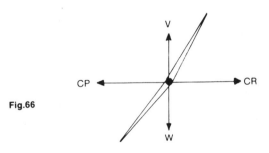

Fig.66

The best way to understand this force is to imagine how a stone whirled around your head on a string is constantly trying to fly off but is held by the string. Centrifugal reaction is the force that keeps the string taut as long as the whirling continues with adequate speed.

Next imagine you are seated in a 'Chair-o-plane' at the fairground. Whilst at rest your weight acts vertically down through the seat.

As the car is set in motion it moves outwards from rest and continues to do so as long as speed is increasing.

Now think about your body as all this is going on. You are pressed further and further into the seat until you cannot move even if you want to; in other words it is as if your weight has increased enormously. In fact you are being subjected to the combination of your own weight and centrifugal reaction. (Fig.67)

The combination or resultant of the two forces CR and W is the diagonal of the parallelogram they can form. The force (or reaction) represented by

48

Fig.67

the diagonal acts straight through the seat at whatever angle you find yourself and it is known as **Loading** (LG). (Fig.68)

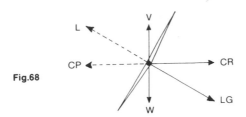

Fig.68

In fact at 60° of bank the loading is equivalent to x2, which means you feel
twice as heavy as you really are.

* From Fig.68 we can now arrive at a conclusion. Since CR = CP and
W = V, then it is obvious that LG must = L.

Hence, when lift is increased to make a balanced turn the loading will go
up at the same rate. Referring back to Fig.64 and, taking the lift increases
at the different angles depicted therein, another table can be produced
which translates into the 'weight' of the pilot for the same situations. On
this occasion L is replaced by LG.

Table 3

	Loading Factor		Pilot Weight		Actual Loading
Level Flight	1.0	x	168 lbs	=	168 lbs
At 15° bank	1.04	x	168 lbs	=	175 lbs
At 30° bank	1.16	x	168 lbs	=	195 lbs
At 60° bank	2.0	x	168 lbs	=	336 lbs

**

Manoeuvring and Loading

A few final points to learn about the turn as a manoeuvre and about loading are as follows:

– To produce the lift required to maintain a steep turn could require increased airspeed that is well beyond the aeroplane's power to produce. The outcome can be a stall and spin if you attempt it – due to increased induced drag.
– It is not only the pilot 'weight' that increases with loading. The whole aeroplane undergoes the stress. Increase the loading beyond the aeroplane's design limit and it can break up in mid-air.
– Loading is not only increased in a turn but in such manoeuvres as a loop, being particularly high in the pulling out at the bottom.

Manoeuvring Speed

So far we have looked at loading in the sense of being careful not to induce manoeuvres which over-stress the aeroplane.

Unfortunately nature can create situations whereby loads can be induced over which you have no control.

The weather can be very fickle and unforgiving in the form of turbulence, where violent gusts can exist which strike with alarming rapidity and with the force of a sledge-hammer.

When the sea is really rough the sailor hauls in the sails to minimise the area exposed to the wind. This move also slows down the boat so that it meets any adverse force with the minimum impact.

An aeroplane cannot haul in any sails but it can reduce its speed to achieve the same end.

The airspeed at which a given aeroplane is adjudged to be capable of handling rough air is known as its **Manoeuvring Speed** and it should be rigidly adhered to where conditions warrant same.

Ancillary Controls

Apart from controls directly associated with manoeuvres there are other controls available which all contribute to easier and safer flight.

They are flaps, slats, trim tabs, servo tabs, balance and brakes. Although their use may be at present confined to aircraft in the light aeroplane upwards bracket it would be remiss not to consider them in the context of the microlight in view of just how fast progress can be.

Flaps

The safest landing is the one which can be made at the minimum of airspeed with the minimum of landing run. At present you may consider that this is the very area in which the microlight scores; but with some now bordering on the performance of light aeroplanes the problem cannot be ignored.

Maximum lift for minimum airspeed can be obtained from a 'nice fat aerofoil' with plenty of top camber. However, the form drag such a shape would produce precludes any decent cruise speed.

The answer lies in altering the wing shape to produce lift at low speed when the occasion warrants it. This facility is brought about by the use of flaps.

Flaps are movable surfaces which extend downwards into the airflow. They are to be found at the trailing edge of each wing between the root and the aileron.

Although there are different types of flaps they all basically serve the same purpose – to increase lift at low speed. (Fig.69)

Simple Flap   Split Flap

Fig.69   Fowler Flap

When a flap is deployed note how the airflow reacts. Not only does the camber increase – together with a wing area increase in the case of the Fowler flap – but the obstruction in the airflow creates a 'warning' to the air ahead. There is an increase in the airflow going over the top of the wing and the speeding up this undergoes adds to lift already produced by camber. (Fig.70)

Fig.70

The angle to which a flap is deployed is important.

    Small Angle – Small increase in drag
               – Large increase in lift

Large Angle – Large increase in drag
            – Little further increase in lift.

Hence you have small angles of flap associated with take-off and large angles in the landing configuration.

Slats

Another way of increasing lift at low speed is to delay the stall beyond the point at which it would normally happen; to permit a greater angle of attack, and thereby a lower airspeed, without lift breaking down.

This situation can be achieved by channelling the airflow through a gap at the leading edge of the wing which speeds up that flow and thus increases lift (Venturi effect). Also, by virtue of the angle at which it is directed on to the wing, there is a delay in the breakdown of the smooth airflow. (Fig.71)

Fig.71

Wing Stalled   Slat Channels
                                 Air over wing

The device which enables all this to take place is known as a **slat** and the gap it forms is known as a **slot**.

Slats are fixed or movable surfaces found at the leading edge of the wing and are aerofoil in shape. The movable type are usually flush with the leading edge and they are 'sucked' out into the airflow as the airspeed slackens off with the increase in angle of attack which in turn causes the reduction in pressure to allow this to happen. Sometimes the gap or slot is built into the leading edge of the wing as opposed to being a separate surface. Such a wing is called a **slotted wing**. (Fig.72)

Fig.72

Trim Tabs

Should a control surface have to be deployed into the airflow for any length of time the resistance met can prove tiring for the pilot.

The problem is overcome by the use of trim tabs. These are small movable surfaces set in the trailing edge of the main control surfaces. (Fig.73)

Fig.73

If maintaining pitch-up control is becoming tedious the tab is deployed in the opposite direction to the control surface and the air thus deflected exerts a force upwards on the elevator thus easing or removing any effort to maintain the elevator in an up position.

Balance

Purely from an interest point of view and in order to avoid confusion should you ever hear the name there is also another tab called a **servo-tab**.

Control input on a very large aircraft can take quite an amount of strength due to the weight and size of the surfaces. Identical in looks and position with a trim tab, the servo-tab however cannot be moved at will by the pilot. It is fixed so that it will go the opposite way to the control surfaces at all times thus assisting the pilot to move the controls. More often than not you will see the two side by side. (Fig.74a)

Fig. 74

Fig.74(b) shows another method of achieving help in moving heavy controls by means known as a graduated balance or shielded horn control surface hinged so that inset segment protrudes into the airflow which in turn pushes that surface in the direction intended.

Air brakes

The need can arise to slow down and lose height rapidly – maybe to land in the only available field in the vicinity due to an engine failure.

Air Brakes enable one to do just this. They are flat plates inset into the wing about one-third of the chord from the leading edge. When deployed they project up into the airflow and the disturbance they cause destroys lift in their vicinity. Air brakes can be single or in pairs. Single brakes are found only on the upper surface; doubles appearing above and below. (Fig.75)

Brakes retracted

Brakes deployed

Breakdown of lift behind brakes

Fig.75

You will recall an earlier mention of spoilers which are used in place of ailerons (Spoilerons) when deployed singly on one wing or another to initiate bank.

When spoilers are deployed simultaneously they naturally take on the role of air brakes.

Summary

In drawing to a close on this subject of principles of flight there are a few points worthy of emphasis.

– Without sufficient airspeed you cannot fly – you will stall.
– Increased airspeed is vital in turn/bank manoeuvres. The steeper the manoeuvre, the greater the stalling speed.
– A stall near the ground may not leave you with sufficient height in which to regain flying speed.
– A stall off the turn may leave you with even less height in which to recover.

Watch your airspeed and you will be able to enjoy watching it over many happy years of flying.

Power and Ancillaries

Types of Power Plant

A hesitant old dear at an air show once asked. 'Young man, why does your machine have that big fan in the front?' 'Madam' replied the intrepid flyer – 'it's to keep me cool up there.'

'You're pulling my leg sir' – was the sharp retort. 'Maybe' said the pilot thoughtfully – 'But you should see how hot I get when it stops!'

An old chestnut perhaps, but it sums up a lot. An in-depth knowledge of engines is not necessary to become a good pilot. What does matter is knowing what can make them stop so that you are able to take precautions against it ever happening and that is the main purpose of this section.

Few people taking up flying are unaware of the basics in engine operation – that is, the **Four-Stroke Cycle**. (Fig.1)

Induction
 – Inlet valve opens
 Fuel mixture sucked in as piston goes down the cylinder

Compression
 – Inlet valve closes
 – Fuel mixture is compressed at top of cylinder as piston returns up the cylinder

Power
 – Mixture is ignited by spark-plug at the end of the compression stroke
 – Expanding hot gases drive piston back down cylinder imparting power to a drive shaft

55

Exhaust
- Outlet valve opens
- Burnt gases escape assisted by piston returning up the cylinder

The **Two-Stroke Cycle**, very relevant to microlights, does the same thing but much faster. (Fig.2)

Compression/
Induction
- Fuel mixture already induced into top of cylinder is compressed as piston goes up
- Simultaneously a new supply of fuel mixture is induced through inlet into crankcase

Power/Exhaust
- Mixture is ignited by spark-plug at the end of the compression stroke
- Expanding hot gases drive piston back down cylinder imparting power to drive shaft
- Simultaneously exhaust outlet is exposed allowing burnt gases to escape
- At the same time the by-pass inlet is also exposed and down-going piston expels new fuel mixture from crankcase through by-pass to top of cylinder.

Cylinder Arrangement

Engines with more than one cylinder are described according to their cylinder layout as follows. (Fig.3)

In each of the above cases you can see that the cylinders have fins around them which dissipate heat into the airflow.

Sometimes a fan is used to blow air over the hot cylinders as well as relying on the airflow.

Either way, such engines are known as **Air Cooled**.

Cylinders can be enclosed in a sealed jacket or casing containing water

In-Line
upright

In-Line
inverted

Radial

Horizontally
opposed

Fig.3

or other specified liquids. The heat is dissipated through a radiator as in a car and the engine in this case is described as **Liquid Cooled**.

Cylinders which become too hot can lead to an engine seizure. It is therefore essential not to modify your motor in a manner that in any way shields a cylinder from the airflow.

Useful additions can be instruments such as a **cylinder head temperature gauge (CHT)**, whose function is self evident by its name, an exhaust gas temperature gauge (EGT). Both will give a warning of impending problems.

Lubrication

A four-stroke engine is lubricated by a separate oil system where oil is pumped to all the vital moving parts.

Never assume you have enough oil. Always carry out a physical check. Just enough is not enough; never take off without the oil tank being fully topped up.

The two-stroke engine lubricates itself as it runs. Oil is mixed with the fuel – petrol in this case – in carefully measured proportions such as 50 parts fuel to 1 part of oil. The ratio here is said to be 50:1.

Pay particular attention to the engine manufacturers handbook as to the ratio required. Mistakes in this area can be costly.

It goes without saying that the correct grade of oil should always be used. Care should be taken to avoid mixing different based oils.

Fuel

Light aeroplanes with their four-stroke engines normally use aviation fuel – AVGAS as it is called. This fuel is available at all main aerodromes and some private landing strips. The filler source for AVGAS will be coloured RED.

As a matter of interest Jet Fuel source points are coloured BLACK.

AVGAS is much more expensive than ordinary car petrol and obtaining it also calls for visiting an aerodrome with all the attendant charges this implies.

After some years of experimentation and trials, motorcar fuel – MOGAS – is now permitted for use in certain nominated aero-engines. However, care is needed in the use of same. The problem that gave concern earlier was the possibility of a constituency breakdown at altitude.

Supplies of MOGAS should only be drawn from a source where the intended use is understood and consistency of specification can be assured. At an airfield a MOGAS source point is also RED.

Drawing supplies from any old garage you come across cannot guarantee the required consistency will be there – particularly as it is changed according to the season.

Two-strokes are fortunately less demanding and drawing petrol from a garage and mixing in the oil oneself is the norm. This is just as well for microlight aeroplanes whose activity is from ordinary fields usually far removed from aerodromes.

Fuel Problems

With the emphasis being on 'trouble-shooting' we will now look at the problems that can arise in a fuel system.

Amount of fuel
– Running out of fuel does happen. Just as you must do with oil, physically check your fuel state prior to take-off – do not rely on gauges alone.

Dirt in fuel
– The easiest way to undergo spontaneous 'engine-off' landing practice is to allow only the smallest particle of grit to find its way into your carburettor fuel jet.

When filling up from cans instead of the pump at an aerodrome re-fuelling point, you run the risk of dirt entering the system.

Ensure you are equipped with the very best filter you can lay your hands on.

Water Contamination
– Water can unintentionally find its way into a fuel system apart from heavy rain taking place during filling.

Should a fuel tank be left empty or partially so for any length of time, the moisture in the air within the tank can condense and the water so formed will settle at the bottom of the tank – water being heavier than petrol.

Some tanks are fitted with a drain cock at the bottom. As part of a preflight check, the pilot releases a sample of fuel into a glass container. Any water present will immediately identify itself at the bottom of the glass.

If water is present, fuel should be drained off until no water is present in the sample.

Because water is heavier than petrol, should there be any other part of the fuel system at a lower point than the tank, then any water found in the tank could also be in that lower part of the system so take no chances.

The risk of condensation can be reduced by keeping tanks full and/or not leaving the aeroplane outdoors all night where the colder night air can cause the condensation.

Venting
– Fuel can only flow through the system if it can be replaced by air as it leaves the tank.

A completely sealed tank will not permit free movement of fuel as, if it could do so, a vacuum (no air area) would be set up and atmospheric pressure outside the tank would at once push the fuel back inside.

To avoid this situation, all tanks are provided with a vent in the filler cap or directly into the tank itself.

Always check that vents are free from obstruction as any blockage could restrict fuel flow into the carburettor.

Carburation

The carburettor is responsible for supplying the correct mixture of fuel and air into the combustion chamber of the cylinder in amounts varying according to the power desired.

Fuel is gravity fed or pumped into a float chamber which, by means of a needle valve closing the fuel inlet, always contains just the right amount of fuel required at a given time. (Fig.4)
Fuel must now be mixed with air to provide the correct mixture. This takes place when air sucked in by piston movement also sucks neat fuel out of the float chamber.

The suction effect is increased because the air passes through a venturi

Fuel flows
into
Float Chamber

Float rises with
intake of fuel
and needle
blocks entry
of fuel

Fig.4

and a reduction in pressure takes place as it speeds up through this restriction (refer back to the section on 'Principles of Flight' for venturi effect).

As the fuel passes from the float chamber to the venturi it flows through a fixed jet. Jets can be of various sizes according to the requirements of a particular engine.

The larger the bore of the jet, the richer the mixture will be. Picture the smallest particle of dirt clogging a jet and you can see why the emphasis is on filtering fuel. Filtering the air intake is also a good move as dirt in a cylinder shortens engine life.

The above operation is depicted in Fig.5.

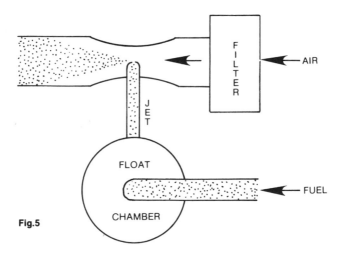

Fig.5

The fuel very quickly vaporises on its way to the combustion chamber to form the highly inflammable mixture needed.

The amount of power is controlled by the amount of mixture admitted into the combustion chamber. This function can be performed in two ways.

On four-stroke engines it is usually in the form of a butterfly valve placed in the path of the mixture on its route from the carburettor to the cylinder. Butterflies can also be found with two-strokes. (Fig.6a)

On many two-strokes the mixture amount admitted is controlled by a plunger which moves up and down in the air intake opening or closing the intake accordingly. Attached to the plunger is a needle valve which regulates the amount of neat fuel admitted to match the amount of air being let through. (Fig.6b)

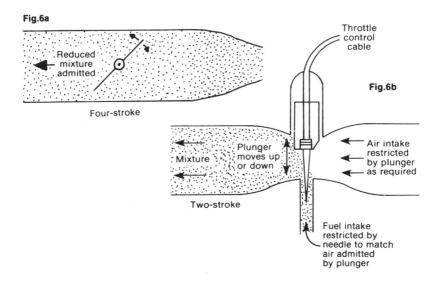

Fig.6a

Throttle control cable

Reduced mixture admitted

Four-stroke

Fig.6b

Plunger moves up or down

Mixture

Two-stroke

Air intake restricted by plunger as required

Fuel intake restricted by needle to match air admitted by plunger

Mixture Problems

Apart from an obstructed jet there are other factors which can influence the efficiency of the fuel mixture introduced into the combustion chamber.

Air Density

If the density of the air should decrease then it means that less air will be flowing through the venturi to mix with the fuel.

This results in a relatively higher proportion of fuel to air or in aviation parlance – a richer mixture.

The outcome of this situation can be a reduction in power – not a nice thought on take off from a short field.

Air becomes less dense as altitude increases or as temperature increases.

Translating this into practical terms it means – watch out when using high altitude airfields and/or taking off in high temperatures.

Humidity

Although not to the same degree as altitude and temperature the humidity of the air can affect density. If the air has a very high water vapour content, it will in fact be less dense than drier air.

Mixture Control

In flight the problem will progress with every foot of altitude you gain as you climb into less dense air.

To a certain extent any loss of power through rich running can be combated by fitting mixture control.

This control reduces the amount of fuel introduced into the venturi so that correct proportions are maintained between fuel and air.

This process is known as 'leaning off' the mixture. However, be careful in creating too lean a mixture. Fuel has a cooling effect and if it is not present in sufficient amounts the engine will begin to 'run hot' and the possibility of a piston seizure is introduced.

The process of leaning off as you climb has its limits. In reducing the amount of fuel to match the reduced amount of air due to less density, you are ending up with an overall less dense mixture which in turn produces less power. Short of fitting a supercharger to ram the required amount of air into the system you will find that every engine reaches the stage where it is no longer producing enough power to sustain flight. However, we are now talking of altitudes way outside the normal environment of microlight or light aircraft.

Carburettor Icing

In talking about fuel mixture we seem to have made some incursions into the realms of meteorology with all the references to air density and humidity.

Discussing carb-icing as it is familiarly known must also be along the same lines.

Cause

When pressure decreases, so does temperature. Also, when evaporation takes place, temperature drops.

In a carburettor the decrease in pressure brought about by the venturi, coupled with the evaporation of fuel as it enters the airflow, both combine to bring about a sharp drop in temperature which can be as much as 33° Celsius in a fraction of a second.

If the drop should take the temperature in the carburettor to below 0°C, which is freezing point, then any water particles produced by condensation due to cooling can at once turn to ice.

The ice can build up in sufficient amounts to restrict the intake of mixture into the cylinder to the extent that not only is power lost but there could be a complete engine failure. (Fig.7)

Fig.7

Conditions favourable for Carb-Icing

If the outside air temperature is well below freezing point any condensation will be straight into ice crystals which will not adhere to the interior of the intake but be ingested into the combustion chamber thus presenting no problem.

There will be no problem either on days when the air is very dry when there is insufficient water vapour to be condensed.

However, conditions conducive to carb-icing are far from infrequent. It can occur any time the air is moist enough and the outside temperature is between –7° and 21°C.

Risk is at a peak during low or closed throttle settings. Reducing this risk will be discussed shortly.

Indications of Carb-Icing

The first indication, if you have a fixed pitched propeller, will be a drop in rpm (engine revolutions per minute) as the mixture intake is restricted.

Later will come a roughness in engine running.

Carb Heating

This is an anti-icing device whereby hot air from the engine is diverted into the venturi so that the resulting mixture ends up above freezing point.

The pre-heated mixture can also melt existing ice which has formed before the carb heating control was applied – providing the accumulation is not too great.

On introducing carb heat make sure the control is full on; partial application can worsen the situation. Results will not necessarily be immediate so be patient and resist the temptation to take it off too soon. It will take time for the ice to melt.

Another form of carb heating is that of diverting hot air from the engine to flow around the carburettor itself. This is intended to warm the component in total but it is not so effective as introducing hot air direct into the venturi.

Problems with Carb Heating

Cures are not without cost. Introduce warm air which is less dense and you end up with a mixture which is less dense. This means a loss in power and a further drop in rpm.

As the ice clears there will be a rise in rpm which will often be accompanied by intermittent rough running as the engine swallows the ice.

When the control is taken off and all ice is gone, the rpm will rise to a higher setting than before its application and the engine will run smoothly.

Because low or closed throttle settings increase the risk of carb-icing, do watch out when descending from height with an idling engine. If you suspect conditions are ripe for carb-icing make sure you open up the throttle periodically for a few seconds. This will ensure you are keeping some heat available to use from an engine which would otherwise be cooling fast.

Finally make sure that carb heat control is not applied on take-off and landing when the availability of full power is critical. However, if a maker's handbook tells you otherwise then naturally you must abide by its instructions.

Ignition

Having carefully nursed the correct mixture all the way to the combustion chamber, it is now time to blow it up!

In actual fact the process is one of progressive burning but at very high speed.

Ignition is the job of a spark-plug which fires just prior to the piston reaching the top of the cylinder so that the maximum impact from detonation of the mixture takes effect as the piston commences its downward stroke.

The spark is generated by an electrical discharge jumping from one electrode to another. The gap between the electrodes is critical so always ensure it is that laid down by the manufacturers.

Too small a gap and the spark may be insufficient to ignite the mixture. Too large and the discharge may not have the strength to jump it – hence no spark. (Fig.8)

Temperature and mixture play an important part in the efficient operation of a plug.

Too low a temperature and/or a rich fuel mixture can cause a carbon deposit to build up between the electrodes.

| Too small
Spark small | Too large
no Spark | Correct
right Spark |

Too high a temperature can damage the electrodes apart from other damage to piston and cylinder.

In a two-stroke engine an added problem can be the oil content in the mixture. If burning is inefficient the electrodes can become wet coated in oil and this insulates them thus preventing a spark – making starting difficult.

This problem is magnified if the cylinder is of the inverted format. The unburnt oil falls into the plug and floods it.

Should you be running in a new engine at an initially higher oil to fuel ratio – say 30:1 instead of 50:1 then with an inverted engine you may find it best to remove the plug after flight and allow residual oil to drip out. If you do not follow this course of action you may find it impossible to start the engine.

Finally, damp can play havoc with plug leads. Often this problem can be overcome by spraying with a proprietary liquid spray, but check that they are worth spraying. Replacement may be what is really needed.

Dual Ignition

Four-stroke engines used in aeroplanes normally have two spark-plugs per cylinder – each being fired by a separate magneto.

Having two sparks in each cylinder ensures maximum burning of the mixture and therefore maximum power for a given throttle setting.

Also, having two of everything means there is a back-up system if one of the two should go wrong.

Prior to take-off each magneto is tested on its own as well as both together.

There will be an acceptable drop in rpm when the engine is running on one magneto as only one out of the two plugs in each cylinder will be firing and therefore power output will not be so great.

Should this drop exceed the acceptable drop laid down for the particular type of engine then you have a problem – either with a plug or the magneto itself.

Some two-stroke engines have two plugs per cylinder but they are both fired from a common source. The benefit of a twin spark is enjoyed and also the back up facility should one fail. However, if anything goes wrong with the magneto then your prowess as a glider pilot comes to the fore.

Master Switch

The definition 'master switch' may give the impression that it controls everything – that nothing will work when it is 'off'. This is not true; it controls the battery and therefore all that depends on this power source and in some cases the alternator or generator.

It does not affect the engine or its primary system – a propeller swing can still start an engine even if the master switch is 'off'.

Ignition Switch

The ignition switch controls the firing – or not – of the engine and it does so in what may seem to be an odd sort of way. It does so by being totally ineffective when in the 'on' position thus allowing firing of plugs to occur.

When switched 'off' it starts to perform its function of earthing the coil or primary windings of the magneto so that the engine cannot fire.

Fire Hazard

When fuel mixture and ignition get together there is always a risk of fire.

In the event of fire the fuel system should be turned 'off' at once along with the ignition switch.

However, should the fire be in the engine you should delay switching off the ignition. By doing so the engine will continue to operate and use up the fuel remaining in proximity to the fire.

When the residual fuel is used up the ignition switch should be turned to 'off' and hopefully the fire will die down with there being no fuel to burn.

Exhaust System

The exhaust system is the means whereby the burnt gases in the combustion chamber are expelled into the air from the engine.

Vital to the system is the silencer as without it the noise would be un-bearable.

With a two-stroke engine the noise potential can be very considerable. Not only does it run at a much higher rpm than a four-stroke but emission of exhaust is at twice the rate due to its operating cycle.

Silencers are carefully designed to match the engine so modifications are out unless approved by the makers.

Unburnt oil in a two-stroke mixture can clog up holes in a silencer and restrict the exhaust gas flow. This can cause back pressure leading to a reduction in power.

Again, always ensure you use the right mixture so as to minimise this possibility.

The Propeller

A propeller is no more than a revolving aerofoil generating lift which pulls or pushes the aeroplane through the air.

The principle is depicted below in Fig.9.

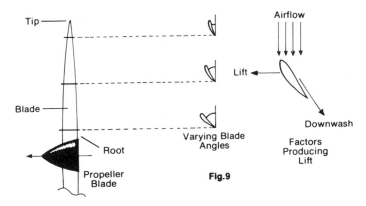

Fig.9

Notice how the angle of the propeller blade progressively lessens from the root to the tip.

Lift increases with both airspeed and angle of attack. To ensure the 'lift' force produced is uniform from root to tip for given propeller revolution, the angle of the blade is—

– Higher at the root where blade speed is lowest
– Lower at the tip where blade speed is highest.

Propeller Arrangement

There are two propeller arrangements to consider – tractor and pusher.

The first pulls the aeroplane through the air; the other pushes as the name implies.

Tractor

The tractor format has certain points worth noting. The airflow from the propeller – slipstream as it is called – increases the airspeed over the inboard surfaces of the wings. This produces extra lift in that area, but be careful

67

that the outboard surfaces do not stall whilst you are making use of the
'inboard bonus' at low airspeed. (Fig.10)

Fig.10

Snags with this form of layout are the increased airflow around the pilot's
face in an open cockpit – unless there is a well-designed windscreen – and
visibility can be impaired somewhat.

Pusher

The tractor snags disappear in this format but so does the increased lift.

The effect is most marked in the sensitivity of control by the tail unit
surfaces of rudder and elevator – but, only as long as power is applied.
(Fig.11)

Fig.11

Propeller Care

Maximum efficiency demands a smooth running perfectly balanced propeller.

The slightest imbalance will at once introduce vibration and along with this comes the loosening of nuts, screws and so forth but more importantly – fatigue.

There is every chance that the cause of imbalance will be damage to a blade.

Taxying over rough ground will see small stones quickly sent up into the propeller arc. Even mud or soft earth will damage high revving blades.

Propellers are often protected to a certain extent by metal or plastic sheeting around the leading edge of the blades.

Apart from imbalance caused by nicks or wear on blades it must be remembered that the propeller at high speed is very brittle and will easily crack if not totally break up on contact with the smallest of objects.

Examine your propeller regularly and thoroughly and any signs of undue wear or cracks must be treated as highly suspect.

Propellers made up of laminated layers of wood must be examined for the possibility of de-lamination taking place where layers are joined.

Propeller Failure

You will be left in no doubt if your propeller fails – the engine will run away to highly unacceptable revs. Damage can be caused to the engine if power is not shut down quickly enough together with selecting 'Ignition Off' the instant it happens. Vibration will be very great.

Before adopting a high speed glide, a cursory glance round and check on controls should be carried out in case damage has been caused to the structure of the aeroplane. If you even suspect such damage, keep airspeed down to a minimum to ease loading on the machine as it descends for a forced landing.

Fitting

Contrary to some beliefs, fitting a propeller the wrong way round will not see you disappearing into reverse on starting up.

What you will experience is a decline in thrust as the effect of camber on the blade in producing lift will be lost. (Fig.12)

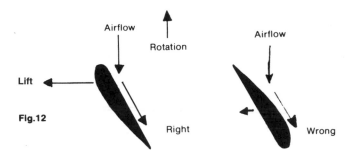

Fig.12

Reduction Gear

We have touched on the fact that the propeller tip travels very much faster than the root.

In fact, a 36 inch diameter propeller at 6500 rpm is bordering on supersonic speed at the tip in travelling at some 735 mph.

That tip only has to go supersonic (760 mph at sea level) to create the most unacceptable noise as it goes through the 'sound barrier'.

Also, as mentioned before, a propeller at high speed is in its most brittle state and susceptible to damage from the least thing in its path – apart from any existing defects which may have weakened it.

Both problems can be eased by slowing the speed of the propeller but in such a way that there is no loss in thrust.

This is achieved by means of reduction gear where the direct drive engine revolutions are reduced to less than half at the point of propeller drive.

The thrust can be maintained – and sometimes increased – by using a larger propeller.

The format of reduction drive as opposed to direct drive is shown in Fig.13 below.

Fig.13

The mechanism of reduction gear on most microlight two-stroke engines has been through the medium of pulleys and belts – the belts being V shaped or toothed like a cog.

Light aeroplane four-stroke engines and more sophisticated microlight two-stroke ones are fitted with a built-in reduction drive with the drive transmitted through cogs.

The built-in drive does however preclude your altering the ratio by introducing varying size pulleys – an advantage you have with the belt drive format.

Pay particular attention to the correct alignment of pulleys in relation to each other and also to the condition of the belts if you want to avoid trouble.

Belts sometimes slip. Engine mounts usually have adjustable nuts to enable slack to be taken up but this remedy is short-lived if the belts are worn.

Slipping belts are readily noticed when swift applications of power bring about increased engine rpm but no increase in propeller thrust. When this comes on in mid-flight you can combat the problem by making any increases in power a very gentle operation in terms of throttle movement; once on the ground, the problem must be rectified before further flight takes place.

Tyre Care/Wheels/Heavy Landings

Tyres tend to become overlooked as they are not vital to flight; however, on take-off and landing they are critical.

Superficial nicks and cuts or scoring may not seem too much of a problem but among them may be a deep one which renders that tyre unfit for use.

Certainly any tyre with the casing exposed must be changed at once. However, baldness in a tyre designed specifically for aircraft is acceptable to a certain degree but not for any length of time. Maintaining correct pressure goes without saying.

Whilst on the subject of wheels it is worth mentioning the effect a grass surface can have – particularly where the diameter is small.

As grass grows it will have a progressive effect on your take-off run by lengthening it – more so if it is wet. Given the small fields that a microlight can use makes watching this point essential. If your propeller begins to look as if they had been dipped in green dye you can assume the grass is too long and you are becoming more of a lawn mower than an aeroplane.

Mud or newly mown hay can play havoc if you have fitted spats – they clog up easily and can be better than brakes being applied at the wrong moment.

Finally, still on the subject of wheels, a word on heavy landings. Such occurrences happen to everyone and human nature makes many pilots relieved that no one saw them!

Such an attitude could not be more dangerous. A quick cursory glance at the wheels, the straightening of the odd tube and into the air once more could mean serious problems.

The shock of a heavy landing may break an under-carriage – in a way this is a good thing. It will mean the wheels could well have absorbed the entire shock.

On the other hand, if they are reasonably intact you must ask yourself – where did the shock go? It has most certainly been transmitted up through the remainder of the airframe.

So, never hide your heavy landings. Assume that damage has been done and ensure an inspection is carried out on all areas which could be affected before you fly again. Incidentally, it is a legal requirement that you enter such incidents in your aircraft log book where they can be noted on inspection.

Sailcloth

With the advent of the Dacron/aluminium technology which is so prevalent in microlight aeroplanes it was initially boasted that the Dacron had an indefinite life.

In fact, the average sailcloth used can have a very long life as long as it is not left exposed to sunlight over any length of time.

The ultra-violet content of daylight causes gradual deterioration to cloth and stitching. An immediate and obvious sign is fading of colour.

Deliberate tests for any weakening is to press your thumb down on the surface and if an indentation remains then you could have a problem.

Again, drawing the back of your thumbnail along the stitching will tell a tale. If it breaks down into a powder it is on its way out.

One way or another, if you have any doubt at all then consult a sail-maker. After all, it is the only means by which you are able to descend from a height at your own discretion. If the cloth should fail, your rate of descent will be that of a discontented breeze-block!

With regard to the powered parachute, the canopy can react adversely to sunlight in the same way as the sailcloth can degrade on a normal micro-light aeroplane; it should be stowed away in a bag when not in use. A wet canopy should be thoroughly dried before being stowed away.

The suspension and control lines on a canopy can be susceptible to chafing so they should be frequently inspected for damage; also all connector links should be frequently inspected and tightened prior to flight if found to be loose.

Corrosion

Another means by which an aeroplane can deteriorate. A watch should be kept for corrosion – particularly around nuts and bolts and flying wires.

Time may account for corrosion in many cases but it can be considerably accelerated in others by exterior factors such as spillage of acid from a battery.

Such acid coming into contact with the aeroplane or rubber tyres should be swiftly washed down in some neutralising solution such as sodium-bicarbonate.

Conclusion

It was said at the beginning of this section that your knowledge needs to be such that you prevent problems rather than be an expert in putting them right after they have occurred.

Digest what you have just read and you will fly more confidently and safely.

Air Law

Introduction

The sky may give the appearance of being empty. In reality it is very much occupied by considerable traffic moving at a variety of speeds ranging from nil to supersonic.

The body responsible for civil flight in the United Kingdom is the Civil Aviation Authority (CAA). The Authority is responsible to Parliament for the smooth, safe operation of such flight and it concerns itself not only with the safety of pilots, passengers and aeroplanes but also with the safety of those on the ground over whom they fly.

Microlight flying is a relative newcomer to the aviation scene compared with other forms of flying. The simpler aeroplanes and minimal operational requirements therefore merited amendments to existing rules in order that the sport could function in a sensible manner.

The amendments have not only taken into consideration the safety aspects, but have made the attainment of a pilot's licence a less forbidding procedure. For example, the introduction of a 'restricted' licence caters for the would-be flyer who simply wishes to fly locally with no aspirations 'to boldly go where no man has gone before' – in other words, one who does not wish to go cross-country flying to any great extent.

In consequence, there are many aspects of the Air Navigation Order to which the microlight pilot and aeroplane owner must conform but which may not appear in most other aviation text books on the subject.

European harmonisation of aviation procedures is taking place under the body known as the Joint Aviation Authority (JAA) who make recommendations to the Commission in Brussels.

So far microlights (or ultralights as they are often referred to in many other countries – particularly the USA) remain untouched by these deliberations except for peripheral matters where there could be a relationship with light aircraft. However, a JAA committee has discussed an increase in weight and a change of the name of 'ultralight' as possibilities for future investigation.

The newcomer in the form of the FLPFM does not come under full regulation and the pilot does not require to have a licence. However, there are definite areas within air law with which an FLPFM pilot must conform and these are shown in the chapter on these machines.

In the meantime digest what you need to know to obtain that coveted licence be it on a microlight or a powered parachute which comes under the same category.

Current Definition of a Microlight

First we will look at the current definition of a microlight. It is

— any one- or two-seat aeroplane whose
— maximum total all-up weight authorised at take-off (MTWA) does not exceed 390 kg whose
— wing loading shall not exceed 25 kg per square metre at MTWA and whose
— fuel content does not exceed 50 litres.

* At present a proposed common Joint Aviation Authority (JAA) definition is being discussed but it has yet to be agreed and accepted as a Joint Airworthiness Requirement (JAR) for Europe. In fact it may not come into being during the lifetime of this edition of the *MPH*. However, the definition put forward by the UK and under review at present is as follows:

> Max All-Up Take-off Weight   –   450 kg 2-Seat
> –   300 kg 1-Seat
> Stall Speed not exceeding 65 kph (35 kt 41mph)
> Wing Loading not exceeding 25 kg per sq metre

There are likely to be additional, more detailed, points but they are best left until this common JAA definition has been finalised.

Note: The UK may introduce the new definition prior to formal ratification by the JAA. **

Aeroplane Airworthiness

All microlight aeroplanes come under CAA airworthiness regulations. It is essential that you know the basics of this legislation if you intend to purchase your own machine.

Before any documentation can be processed, the aeroplane must be registered with the CAA and have the allocated letters displayed on its surfaces.

The CAA will only send an airworthiness document to the name appearing in the UK Register of Aeroplanes.

Should you wish to take your microlight abroad on holiday you must apply to the CAA for a dispensation.

Since the 1st April 1988, all microlight aeroplanes must be in possession of a Noise Certificate issued by the CAA on behalf of the Department of Transport.

There are three categories of aeroplane for airworthiness purposes.

Type Approved Aeroplanes

Are all microlight aeroplanes which
> first flew **after** the 1st January 1984

They must have gained CAA Type Approval for their designs and the manufacturers producing same must have CAA Company Approval.

In order to fly legally, a Type Approved aeroplane must be in possession of a **Type Approved Permit to Fly**.

Type Accepted Aeroplanes

Are all microlight aeroplanes which first flew
> **Prior** to the 1st January 1984 if *over* 70 kg empty weight
>
> or
>
> **Prior** to the 1st January 1987 if *under* 70 kg empty weight

must have gained Type Acceptance and have a **Type Accepted Permit to Fly** to fly legally.

Type Accepted aeroplanes are machines which were flying before the introduction of legislation but on investigation of their engineering, flight performance and track record, there has been sufficient evidence shown to warrant them continuing to fly subject to any necessary modification.

Home Built Aeroplanes

Aeroplanes constructed by the owner from scratch or from a kit require a **Home Built Permit to Fly** to fly legally.

Validation of Airworthiness Documents

Airworthiness documents are validated as follows
Type Approved/
Type Accepted or Home Built
Permit to Fly – **Annually** – subject to a satisfactory inspection by an approved Inspector and followed by a satisfactory check flight by an approved Check Pilot.
Inspections – Must be carried out against a laid down schedule and any specific documents pertinent to the aeroplane type.
Check Flights – Must be authorised by an approved Inspector and be

carried out against a laid down schedule by an approved Check Pilot.

– Must be carried out **no later than 30 days after the inspection**.

Applications – Must be submitted to the BMAA **within 30 days of any check flight**.

Issues – A Permit to Fly of any sort must have been validated before legal flight can take place.

Modifications – No modification may be made to a microlight aeroplane **without** the approval of the CAA or a body approved by the CAA.

Pilot Medical Requirements

So much for the aeroplanes; now we look at you, the pilot.

Before you can obtain a flying licence you must be in possession of a current medical certificate.

This certificate also acts as a licence for you to go solo whilst undergoing flight training but you are not allowed to carry passengers on the strength of it.

It requires renewal according to your age at the following times.

Less than 40 years of age	–	5 years
40 and over but less than 50	–	2 years
50 and over but less than 70	–	1 year
Over 70 years of age	–	6 months

If you are over 37 years of age but under 40 when issued with your certificate, it will need renewing on your 42nd birthday.

No medical is required. In this case the certificate is in the form of a 'Declaration of Fitness' (FCL 150/AB) countersigned by your own doctor or a CAA Authorised Medical Examiner (AME).

Should you suffer injury or illness which precludes your ability to act as a pilot for 20 days or more, you are obliged to report the fact to the CAA. Your medical certificate will be deemed to be suspended from the date of occurrence until such time as you are examined in respect of the particular problem and certified as once more medically fit.

Microlight Licences

There are two types of licence.

– **Private Pilot's Licence (Aeroplanes) Microlight**
– **Private Pilot's Licence (Aeroplanes) Powered Parachutes**

They are normally referred to as PPL (M) and PPL (PP) respectively and within each type there is a further sub-division. Qualifications and limitations are as follows.

PPL (M)
Restricted
With
Operational
Limitations

(a) A minimum of 15 hours flying instruction on a microlight aeroplane of which 7 hours must be solo. The solo hours must be completed within the 9 month period prior to the date of application for a licence.

(b) Pass a General Flying Test (GFT) carried out by an authorised instructor holding an Examiner (X) Rating within the 9 months period prior to the date of application for a licence.

(c) Pass examinations in Aeroplanes Technical, Air Law, Human Performance Limitations, Navigation and Meteorology within the 12 month period prior to the date of application for the licence.

(d) Flying on a 'Restricted' licence means that you cannot fly
   – When the surface wind is 15 knots or above
   – When the cloud base is below 1000 ft
   – When the in-flight visibility is below 10 km
   – Outside a radius of 8 nm from your take-off point.

(e) You cannot carry passengers until you have logged at least 25 hours flight time on a microlight aeroplane, of which at least 10 hours must have been as Pilot-in-Command and your log book has been endorsed by an Examiner to verify those hours.

Unrestricted
Without
Operational
Limitations

(a) In addition to requirements (a), (b) and (c) for the PPL (M) Restricted.

(b) Obtain a further 10 hours flying time on a microlight aeroplane of which at least 5 hours must be navigation training under instructor supervision.

(c) During the navigation training, complete 2 solo cross-country flights of at least 40 nautical miles (nm) each, over different routes.

(d) During each cross-country flight an out-landing must be made at a site at least 15 nm from the take-off point.

A pilot may go straight for the Unrestricted Licence from the start in which case the navigational cross-country requirements must also be completed within the 9 month period prior to applying for the licence.

PPL (PP)

Restricted
With
Operational
Limitations

(a) A minimum of 4 hours flying instruction on a powered parachute aeroplane of which at least one hour must be solo.

(b) During the period of flight instruction carry out not less than 25 take-offs and full-stop landings of which 6 must be solo.

(c) The above hours and flights must be completed within the 9 months period prior to applying for a licence.

(d) Pass a General flying Test (GFT) carried out by an authorised Instructor holding an Examiner (X) appointment within the 9 month period prior to the date of application for a licence.

(e) Pass examinations in Aeroplanes Technical, Air Law, Human Performance Limitations, Navigation and Meteorology within the 12 month period prior to the date of application for the licence.

(f) Flying on a 'Restricted' licence means that you cannot fly
   - When the surface wind exceeds 10 knots
   - When the cloud base is below 1000 ft
   - When the in-flight visibility is below 10 km
   - Outside a radius of 8 nm from your take-off point

(g) You cannot carry passengers until you have logged at least 15 hours flight time of which at least 10 hours must have been as Pilot-in-Command (PIC) and your log book has been endorsed by an Examiner to verify those hours.

Unrestricted
Without
Operational
Limitations

(a) In addition to requirements (a), (b), (c), (d) and (e) for the PPL (PP) Restricted,

(b) Obtain a further 11 hours flying time on a powered parachute aeroplane of which at least 5 hours must be navigation training under instructor supervision.

(c) During the navigation training, complete 2 solo cross-country flights of at least 25 nm each over different routes and to different sites.

(d) During each cross-country flight an out-landing must be made at a site at least 10 nm from the take-off point.

A pilot may go straight for the Unrestricted licence without operational limitations from the start in which case the solo navigational cross-country requirements must also be completed within the 9 month period prior to the date of application for a licence.

Keeping a Licence Valid

Apart from being in possession of a current declaration of fitness to keep your licence valid, there are naturally flying requirements to be fulfilled.

Your flying log book must be stamped by an Examiner every 13 months confirming that you have flown at least 5 hours of which 3 must have been as P.1 (Pilot-in-Command). The other 2 hours may be dual with an appropriate instructor or examiner for the purpose of becoming P.1 again.

Should you not have achieved the requisite hours within the time laid down, you will be required to undergo a flight test by an Examiner within 26 months from the date of your last Certificate of Test. On successful completion of the flight test you will have your log book stamped with a Certificate of Test.

Until this test has been carried out, you cannot fly without being under the supervision of an instructor.

Privileges of a PPL (M) or (PP)

The privileges concern the limitations under which you may fly any aeroplane within the group covered by your licence. They largely concern the rules and the flight conditions pertaining to them. In aviation as a whole these can appear to be quite complex.

However, you need only be concerned with the rules under what are called **Visual Flight Rules (VFR)** and flight conditions called **Visual Meteorological Conditions (VMC)**. But even within these rules there are limitations imposed on you. So, to save you having to sort the matter out for yourself; here in a nutshell is what you must do.

(a) Always be clear of cloud and in sight of the surface.

(b) Always have an in-flight visibility of not less than 3 kilometres.

(c) Always when above 3000 feet AMSL (above mean sea level)
   - have an in-flight visibility of not less than 5 kilometres
   - Never be less than 1500 metres from cloud horizontally
   - never be less than 1000 feet vertically from cloud.

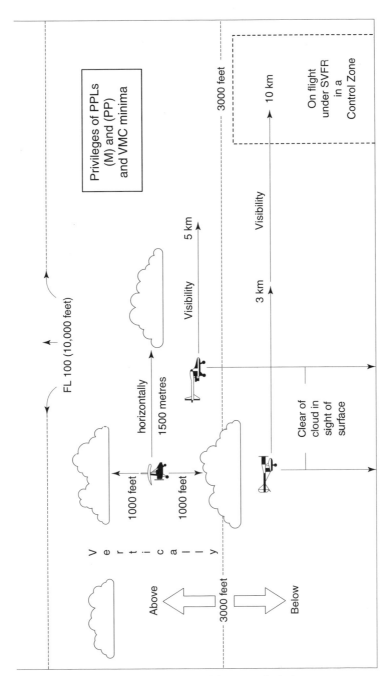

Fig.1. An illustration of the limitations outside controlled airspace.

(d) Note well, all the above rules only apply **outside** controlled airspace; also, if you ever intend going above 10,000 feet AMSL in the distant future – look up the rules when the time comes!

VMC Requirements

Because you are flying VFR, do not be misled if you come across other parts of these rules which seem to allow you to deviate from your privileges – you are not permitted to do so.

You may have noticed that *weather* criteria is defined in a mixture of feet and metres. The main reason for this confliction is that heights are still termed in feet due to the fact that most altimeters worldwide are calibrated thus.

You will also come across definitions which are in feet, kilometres and nautical miles (nm). The latter situation applies to *navigational* data relating to air traffic zones and suchlike.

Apart from the limitations inposed by your licence, the Permit to Fly (PTF) on your aeroplane lays down further limitations to which you must adhere.

Conditions Specific to Permits to Fly

A microlight aeroplane shall not be flown for the purposes of public transport or aerial work, other than aerial work consisting solely of the giving of instruction in flying where the aeroplane is **Type Approved**.

A microlight aeroplane is **not** permitted to overfly an assembly of persons, a congested area, town or settlement at any time – **even at 1500 ft or above**.

A microlight aeroplane is **not** permitted to perform aerobatics at any time. Steep turns not exceeding 60 degrees (unless the aeroplane manual gives a lower figure) and intentional stalls from level flight including a turn in level flight are not considered to be aerobatic manoeuvres.

A microlight aeroplane is not permitted to fly at night.

Personal Flying Log Book

A personal flying log book must be kept by qualified pilots or pupils under training for the purposes of becoming qualified. This log book must be kept available for producing to any recognised authority for a minimum of two years after the date of the last entry.

It must contain particulars of all flights made as a flight crew member or for the purposes of renewing a licence or rating. Flying hours count from the time the aeroplane moves off from rest under its own power for the purposes of undertaking flight to the time it comes to rest on landing and power is switched off.

The particulars to be recorded are:
- Date of flight
- Type of aircraft
- Your capacity as pilot during the flight
- Registration letters of aircraft
- Places of departure and arrival
- Total flight time
- Details of any particular activity, e.g. any training exercises in connection with obtaining a licence
- Particulars of any test/examination taken during the flight

Radio Telephony Licence

As microlights have become more and more advanced in their capability to travel, so the greater is becoming the use of radio. One tip, do remember to call up in good time; if not, you may easily enter a zone or area before receiving your instructions.

The wavebands are crowded with transmissions and this calls for accuracy and brevity in their use. A radio-equipped aircraft is deemed to be a 'radio station' and to operate same requires that you undertake a short course in procedures followed by a simple test of your competency.

On successful completion of the course you will be issued with a **Flight Radio Telephony Operator's Licence**.

Note well – if your radio is a permanently fixed feature of your aeroplane you are responsible for obtaining a licence for the equipment itself as well as the licence for operating same.

UK Airspace

For the microlight pilot the need to know about airspace is mainly for the purposes of knowing where and when to keep away from many parts of it.

Airspace in the UK below Flight Level 245 (24,500 feet) is divided into two **Flight Information Regions (FIRs)** known as the **London FIR** and the **Scottish FIR**.

Above FL245 the same regions are known as **Upper Flight Information Regions (UIRs)**

All airspace is either controlled or uncontrolled. It is further divided into classes of airspace – each with its own set of flight requirements. The following zones and areas are Class A airspace. In controlled airspace there are to be found zones and areas as follows.

Zones and Areas

Control Zone (CTR) – Defined airspace from the surface to a specified altitude (QNH) or flight level (FL). (Covered later on page 87.)

Control Area (CTA) – Defined airspace extending upwards from a specified altitude (QNH) or flight level (FL) to an upper limit expressed as a flight level.

Airway – A control area in the form of a corridor which extends 5 nm either side of a line joining two places at which navigational aids are usually sited.

Each airway has specified vertical limits and has its own letter/number identification code.

Terminal Manoeuvring Area (TMA) – Is the same as a CTA but is the name given to some control areas around selected major aerodromes – for example, the London TMA (LTMA).

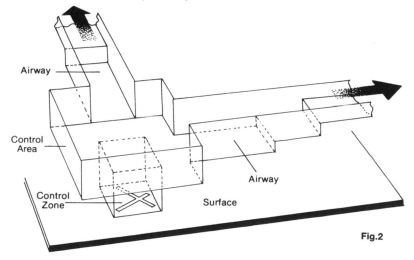

Airway

Control Area

Control Zone

Airway

Surface

Fig.2

Advisory Service Areas

Advisory Area – An area in which a service exists for aircraft requesting separation from other aircraft. The separation can only be given from other aircraft using the service.

Advisory Route – This is an advisory area similar in dimensions to an airway.

Separation service is provided as for an advisory area.

Classes of Airspace

Controlled

Class A – Airways and certain defined CTRs, CTAs and TMAs

Note: Class A airspace only permits flying under Instrument Flight Rules (IFR). (Not applicable to a microlight pilot but covered for interest's sake on page 112.) However, you could fly in a CTR on your licence subject to permission under Special Visual Flight Rules (SVFR). (See below)

Class B – Upper Airspace (above FL245)

Class C – Not allocated at present

Class D – Defined CTRs and CTAs

Class E – As and when defined, for example

The Scottish TMA at and below 6000 feet AMSL

The Belfast TMA

The Scottish CTR outside the Glasgow and Prestwick CTRs

Uncontrolled

Class F – Advisory Routes   Class G – Open airspace

The above classes are depicted on UK aeronautical charts as follows:

Class A ——————   Class B —— —— ——   Class D —— —— ——

Class E — ·· — ·· —   Class F ——— ———   Class G ⌐__⌐__⌐

(As and when allocated) Class C ——— —— —— ———

Note: The above identification markings for airspace are different on the charts of other European States; as yet there is no agreed ICAO standard.

We will now go on to deal with the rules for flying within these classes of airspace and the minimum weather criteria attached to them. Again, these rules are in compliance with agreement reached with the ICAO.

You will recall that inside controlled airspace there can be zones and areas which are "notified" and for which the rules will be different.

Special VFR Flight (SVFR)

The SVFR is a flight where the pilot is given permission to penetrate controlled airspace when the necessary qualifications to do so as a matter of course are not held.

∗ Diverting for a moment, there are additional qualifications where other pilots can operate to lower limits than yourself, such as flying in cloud, in what are known as **Instrument Meteorological Conditions**

(IMC) for which they require an **IMC Rating** on their licence.

Further up the ladder are the pilots who operate not only in IMC conditions but throughout control zones and control areas such as airways where they are constantly under control from the ground. Such pilots are said to be flying under **Instrument Flight Rules (IFR)** for which they must hold an **IFR Rating** on their licence.

There is the **Night Rating** for flying at night (obviously!) with night being defined as between half an hour after sunset to half an hour before sunrise. Sunset and sunrise are defined as being seen at the surface – not from the air. You should recall that a microlight is not permitted to fly at night.

Currently no microlight licence can have any of the above ratings attached to it. Perhaps you can see why this chapter is confining itself in the main only to what you need to know!

So, in all cases SVFR flights can only be made with clearance by an Air Traffic Control (ATC) unit. They take place:

– Within a control zone designated as IFR – or

– in IMC conditions – or

– at night.

Normally, should the authorised route make the rule of 1500 feet above the highest fixed object within 2000 feet impossible to obey then you are absolved from complying with same. **But**, by now, with a knowledge of the limitations imposed on you by your licence and permit to fly, you should have deduced that on an SVFR flight in a microlight you cannot fly at night or in IMC conditions. Also, you cannot fly over any built up area at any time so you cannot be absolved from the 1500/2000 ft rule.

A SVFR flight also absolves you from complying with IFR but it does not absolve you from remaining clear of cloud and in sight of the surface with a minimum in-flight visibility of not less than 10 kilometres. Lower visibility requirements may apply for SVFR flights in certain notified Air Traffic Zones and certain notified access lanes within controlled airspace.

However, do bear in mind that authorisation you may be given does not absolve you from the obligation to be able to 'land clear' as laid down in (b) under 'Low Flying Rules'. (See Page 88)

In flight under VFR the pilot is entirely responsible for separation from other aircraft.

All this limits any SVFR flight you may undertake to passing through a CTR where conditions are such that you are clear of cloud, in sight of the surface and have an in-flight visibility not less than 10 kilometres. It must also be daytime and there must also be no built up area which cannot be avoided. Better than nothing I suppose.

Flight Plans

A flight plan consists of details of a planned flight which is lodged with ATC not less than 60 minutes prior to departure for VFR flight. ATC then notify all concerned but will still require the PIC to 'Book out' on leaving.

Flight plans are usually associated with commercial or IFR flights but a private pilot may file one and in fact is definitely advised to do so if intending to fly more than 10nm off the coast or over mountainous or sparsely populated areas.

Should you be over 30 minutes overdue at your destination, or land at an airfield other than your original destination without informing the latter, then a search and rescue operation will be set in motion.

However, should your take-off and destination be a simple airstrip or an airfield without an Air Traffic Control (ATC) facility operating at the time, no action would be taken on your non-compliance with the flight plan.

A flight plan is mandatory if you intend crossing an international boundary.

Pre-Flight Actions

The Pilot-in-Command (PIC) must always ensure that all conditions in relation to the aeroplane and the planned flight are right in every way and, in case of an emergency, the passengers are aware of what to do and the location of safety equipment.

Aerodrome Traffic Zones – Civil and Military

Many aerodromes lie outside controlled airspace but this does not mean there is no form of procedure. Most of them have their own zones as follows.

Aerodrome Traffic Zone – Extends up to 2000 ft above aerodrome
(ATZ)   level (QFE) and outwards within a
                         radius of 2nm centred on the mid point
                         of the longest runway where the runway
                         length is *less* than 1,850 metres.
                         Otherwise, it is 2½nm.

On no account should entry into an ATZ be made without prior permission given over the radio or by telephone prior to flight.

On permission being granted if you are flying non-radio, keep a sharp look-out for visual signals in the signals area and for light signals which can come from the control tower or a caravan placed near the take-off point on the runway in use.

If you are on radio and just passing through an ATZ, you should report your position and height on entering and leaving the zone.

It is essential to be fully aware of an aerodrome's requirements before flying in.

Military Aerodrome Traffic Zone (MATZ)	– Extended ATZ reaching up to 3000 ft above aerodrome level (QFE) within 5 nm radius of the centre of the aerodrome.
	– can sometimes have a 'stub' or 'Panhandle' projecting from the circle extending from 1000 ft to 3000 ft above ground level (QFE) being 4 nm in width and 5 nm in length.

Some military aerodromes are shown on charts devoid of any MATZ marking. Also, the MATZ itself has no mandatory power.

However, penetration of a MATZ without contacting ATC would be foolhardy in view of the nature of the flying that can take place from such airfields – and anyway the ATZ rules still stand.

Military Low Flying

There are areas in the UK where military low flying can take place up to 2,000 ft AGL, although such activity is usually between 250 and 500 ft AGL. Such areas are not under any control and there is particular need to keep a careful look-out in same.

General Flight Rules

Just as you have the 'highway code' for motoring, so in the air there are rules and signals that have to be obeyed.

A 'flight' is designated to be from engine on to engine off these rules extend to movement on the ground as well.

Reference will occasionally be made to the term 'flying machine'. This is the official description of a power driven heavier than air aircraft.

One point you must remember. Whatever the rules may say it is the pilot in command who is responsible for avoiding a collision when all is said and done. This philosophy also applies regardless of any ATC clearance given.

Low Flying Rules

The public very soon notice a low flying aircraft and their reaction has considerable bearing on the image of the pilot and of flying itself.

The pertinent rules are as follows

(a) An aircraft shall not fly closer than 500 ft to any person, vessel, vehicle or structure.

Exceptions to this rule are:
- Taking off and landing
- Gliders whilst slope soaring
- Performance at an aircraft race, contest or display where the appropriate permission has been obtained.

(b) An aircraft other than a helicopter shall not fly over a congested area such as a city, town or settlement used mainly for residential, industrial, commercial or recreational purposes
- Below a height that would allow it to land clear of the area without danger to people or property in the event of engine failure

or

- At less than 1500 ft above the highest fixed object within 2000 ft, whichever is the higher.

Exceptions to this rule are:
- Taking off and landing
- Flying on an authorised SVFR flight

(c) At a gathering of more than 1000 people no aircraft shall fly
- Over that gathering
- Within 3000 ft of it

Exceptions to this rule are:
- When flying with the appropriate permission of the Authority
- When on route at a reasonable height and in no way being associated with the gathering. You could still be reported on this count but your defence would be good if you could prove no connection with the assembly.

Again you should have deduced that whilst these are the general rules, you still have limitations attached to your Permit to Fly which cannot be ignored.

- Under (a) – If any site requires take-off and landing over a built up area, you *cannot* use that site in a microlight.
  (Do note that the 500 ft rule is not a height stipulation, it is a 'distance from' rule. This is often mis-understood, particularly by the public when complaining.)

- Under (b) – Does not apply to you as you cannot fly over any built up area *at any time* in a microlight.

However, all rules go out the window when action is necessary for the saving of life.

Collision Avoidance and Rights of Way

On Route
- Flying machines must give way to airships, gliders and balloons.
- Airships must give way to gliders and balloons.
- Gliders must give way to balloons.
- An aircraft giving way must avoid passing over, under or crossing ahead of the other aircraft until well clear of it.
- When two aircraft are converging at about the same altitude, the aircraft which has the other on its right must give way. (Fig.3)

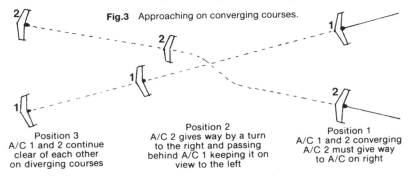

Fig.3 Approaching on converging courses.

Position 3	Position 2	Position 1
A/C 1 and 2 continue clear of each other on diverging courses	A/C 2 gives way by a turn to the right and passing behind A/C 1 keeping it on view to the left	A/C 1 and 2 converging A/C 2 must give way to A/C on right

Notes:

Should the aircraft to the left be towing another aircraft or an object such as a banner, then the one on the right must give way.

In all other respects a flying machine towing another aircraft shall be considered to be a single aircraft under the command of the pilot of the towing aircraft.

- When two aircraft are approaching head on, or nearly so, each must turn right. (Fig.4)

Fig.4 Approaching head on.

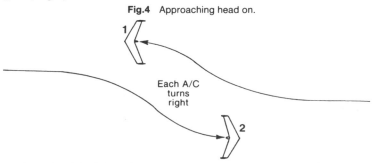

Each A/C
turns
right

- An aircraft with right-of-way should maintain course and speed.
- An aircraft must not fly so close to other aircraft as to create a danger of collision.

– An aircraft overtaking another aircraft shall turn to the right. (Fig.5)

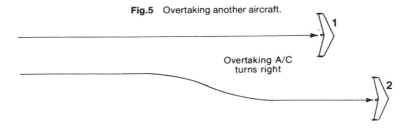

Fig.5 Overtaking another aircraft.

Notes:
This applies whether climbing or descending as well as in level flight.
A glider however may turn right or left.
– An aircraft following a prominent landmark such as a railway, motorway, coastline and so forth should keep such a landmark to its left. (Fig.6)

Fig.6 Following a main ground feature.

Near an Aerodrome

– An aircraft approaching or flying in the vicinity of an aerodrome must conform to the pattern of traffic formed by other aircraft intending to land there.
  Note:
  If unable to do so the aircraft should keep well clear of the airspace in which the pattern is formed.
– All turns should be made to the left unless ground signals state otherwise.
– An aircraft landing or on final approach has right of way over others in flight or on the ground.
– Where two or more aircraft of similar category (e.g. two flying machines) are approaching to land, the lower aircraft has right-of-way.
  Note:
  The lower aircraft must not be cutting in or overtaking another at the time.
– When ATC has given an aircraft a place in the priority for landing this sequence must be adhered to.
– When an aircraft commander is aware that another is making an emergency landing he must give way.

Note:
If this should occur at night he must await further permission to land irrespective of any earlier directions given.

Take-off and Landing
– Take-off must be in the direction indicated by ground signals.
– Landing on a runway which is occupied by other aircraft must not take place unless authorised by ATC.
– Where take-offs and landings are not confined to a runway an aircraft which is landing must leave clear on its left any aircraft which has landed or is landing or is about to take-off.
  Note:
  Any turn must be to the left as long as there is no interference with other traffic.
– A flying machine about to take-off must manoeuvre so as to leave clear on its left any aircraft which has already taken off or is about to do so.
– A flying machine on landing must move clear of the landing area as soon as possible unless ATC says otherwise.
– There are rules about landing and take-off in respect of wake turbulence caused by other aircraft. The official figures are to be found under 'Meteorology' on Page 130.

On the Ground
– Aircraft on the ground must give way to those taking off or landing.
– Aircraft on the ground must give way to any vehicle towing an aircraft.
– Aircraft on the ground have right of way over vehicles.
  Note: The above are in order of priority
– When two aircraft are taxying towards each other head-on, or nearly so, each must turn to the right.
– When two aircraft are converging the one which has the other on its right must give way – avoiding crossing ahead of the other unless passing well clear.
– An aircraft overtaking another aircraft or vehicle must turn to the left and keep out of the way until past and well clear.

Signals

When no radio is carried the Air Traffic Controller will communicate with the aircraft using visual signals.

These signals fall into two broad categories – general and particular.

General signals are those applicable to all users of the aerodrome in question and are to be seen laid out in a 40ft by 40ft hollow white square known as the 'Signals Area'.

Signals in this area should be easily readable by a pilot flying over at 2000 ft and are covered later in this section.

Particular signals are those which are specific to an individual aircraft at a given time. Normally they are made by coloured beams of light emitted from an 'Aldis' type lamp. There are occasions when star shells will be used, fired by a Very pistol.

Signals to an Aircraft on the Ground

Intermittent Green Beam	– You may move on the manoeuvring area and apron.
Continuous Green Beam	– You may take-off
Intermittent Red Beam	– Move clear of landing area.
Continuous Red Beam	– Stop.
Intermittent White Beam	– Return to starting point on aerodrome.

Signals to an Aircraft in the Air

Intermittent Green Beam	– Return to aerodrome – wait for permission to land.
Continuous Green Beam	– You may land.
Intermittent Red Beam	– Do not land – aerodrome not available for landing.
Continuous Red Beam	– Give way to other aircraft and continue circling.
Intermittent White Beam	– Land at this aerodrome after receiving continuous green and after intermittent green proceed to apron.
Red Pyrotechnic or Flare	– Do not land – wait for permission.

Signals from an Aircraft in the Air to an Aerodrome

Red Pyrotechnic or Flare	– Immediate assistance is requested.
Cont. or Int. Green Beam or Green Pyrotechnic	– By night: may I land? – By day: may I land in a different direction to the landing 'T'?
Intermittent White Beam or White Pyrotechnic lights switching navigation or landing lights on and off.	– I am compelled to land

Ground Signals at Aerodromes

Referring now to the 'Signals Area', this is usually situated near the control tower. Signals may be displayed therein or on a mast.

The following are some of the signals which you will come across and a useful means of learning is to colour them in yourself.

Landing prohibited

– A **red** square panel with **yellow** diagonals denotes the aerodrome is unsafe and landing there is prohibited.

Special Precautions

– A **red** square panel with one **yellow** diagonal denotes that the manoeuvring area is poor and special care is needed when landing.

Use Hard Surfaces at all times

– A **white** dumb-bell denotes that the movement of aeroplanes and gliders on the ground is confined to hard surfaces only.

Use only Hard Surfaces for take-off and Landing

– A *white* dumb-bell with **black** strips at right angles to the shaft denotes taking off and landing shall be on hard surfaces but ground movement is not so restricted.

Right Hand circuit

– A **Red** and **yellow** striped arrow along two sides of the signal area and pointing clockwise denotes a right hand circuit is in force.

– A rectangular **green** flag on the mast is an alternative for this signal.

Gliding

– A double **white** cross denotes gliding is in progress. A similar but much larger signal is used to mark the area on the aerodrome to be used only by gliders.

– Two **red** balls on the mast is an alternative to the cross.

– A **yellow** cross denotes the tow-rope dropping area.

Direction of Take-off and Landing

– A **white** 'T' denotes direction of take-off and landing towards the cross-piece of the 'T' unless otherwise authorised by ATC.

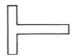

– A **white** disc ahead of the 'T' cross piece indicates that take-off and landing directions may not necessarily coincide.

– A single **black** ball on the mast is an alternative to the white disc ahead of the 'T'.

Landing Area for Light Aircraft
– A **white** letter 'L' denotes a part of the manoeuvring area which shall be used only for the take-off and landing of light aircraft.

– A **red** letter 'L' across a **white** dumb-bell denotes that light aircraft can use runways or areas designated by the **white** 'L'.

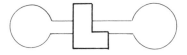

Helicopter Operations
– A **two-metre** high **white** letter 'H' in the signals area denotes that heli-copters can only take-off and land in a designated area.

– A **six-metre** high **white** letter 'H' denotes that area.

Runway Indication
– Two-figure **black** numerals on a **yellow** background denote the runway in use.

Aerodrome Control in Operation
– A checkered **red/yellow** flag on the mast denotes that aircraft can only move on the apron and within the manoeuvring area with the permission of ATC.

Reporting Point
– A **black** 'C' on a **yellow** background denotes this point.

Unserviceable Portion of Runway/taxi-way
– Two or more **white** crosses at 45° to the centre line and not more than 300 metres apart denote the section so marked as unfit for aircraft movement.

Boundaries

Markers/Flags with orange/white stripes are used to mark boundaries of unfit areas. They can also indicate aerodrome boundaries.

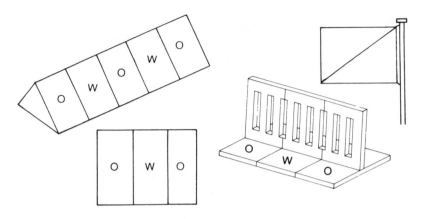

Military/Disused Aerodromes

– **A red** letter 'L' denotes that light aircraft may land on a special area shown by **white** corner markings.

– A **white** cross displayed at the end of the runway denotes that landing is dangerous.

– A **white** cross and a single **white** bar at the end of a runway on a disused aerodrome denotes fitness to land in an emergency only.

– **Yellow** and **black** triangular solid sections denote areas unserviceable due to bad ground, the presence of working parties, stationary vehicles or other obstructions.

– Two vertical **yellow** bars on a **red** square indicate landing areas are serviceable but normal facilities are not available. Land in an emergency only.

– A **red** flag on the mast denotes a left hand circuit.
– A **green** flag on the mast denotes a right hand circuit.

As microlights become more readily accepted at aerodromes, there are additional signs to be taken into consideration.

Marshalling Signals from Marshal to Pilot for Fixed Wing Aeroplanes

Signal	Meaning	
Right or left arm down. Other arm moved across body and extended to position of other marshal	Proceed to guidance from another marshal	
Arms repeatedly moved upward and backward beckoning onward	Move ahead	
Right arm down, left arm repeatedly moved upward and backward. Speed of movement indicates rate of turn	Turn to port (left) or open up starboard engine	

Left arm down, right arm repeatedly moved upward and backward. Speed of movement indicates rate of turn	Turn to starboard (right) or open up port engine	
Arms repeatedly crossed above the head. Speed of movement denotes urgency required	Stop	
Circular motion of the right hand at head level with the left arm pointing to the appropriate engine	Start engines	
Arms extended, the palms facing then swung from the extended position inwards	Chocks inserted	
Arms down, the palms facing outwards then swung outwards	Chocks away	
Either arm and hand placed level with the chest. Then moved laterally with the palm downward	Cut engines	
Arms placed down, with the palms towards the ground then moved up and down several times	Slow down	
Arms placed down, with the palms towards the ground, then either the right or left arm moved up and down indicating that the motors on the left or right side, as the case may be, should be slowed down.	Slow down engine/s on side indicated	

Arms placed above the head in a vertical position	This bay or parking spot	
Right arm raised at the elbow with the arm facing forward	All clear – marshalling is complete	

Distress Signals

For an aircraft in grave or imminent danger needing immediate help or in a situation likely to lead to same
– Over radio telephone (RT) – the call sign 'Mayday' on 121.5 MHz
– Visually – SOS in Morse
      – Succession of single red pyrotechnics at short intervals
      – A red parachute flare
– Sound (other than RT) – SOS
      – Continuous sound made by any means.
For an aircraft in difficulties which compel it to land but not in need of immediate help. Where no RT is available:
– Succession of white pyrotechnics
– Repeated switching on and off of landing lights
– Repeated switching on and off of navigation lights in a manner different to normal flashing lights if this type is fitted.
Where an urgent message needs to be sent concerning the safety of, say, a ship, aircraft, vehicle, property or person within sight of the aircraft
– Over RT – 'PAN'
– Visually – XXX in Morse
– Sound (other than RT) – XXX in Morse

Navigation Lights

At night flying machines and airships display navigation lights at either side which show through 110° from dead ahead – red on the port (left) and green on the starboard (right) side.
    At the tail a single white light shows through 140° when viewed from dead astern – 70° on either side. (Fig.6)
As you can see, one of the lights is visible at all times as the spread covers 360°.
    Careful note of a navigation light and its bearing from you will help to avoid a collision at night.

Red
110°

Green
110°

White
140°

Fig.7

Diagrammatically it is difficult to provide examples of how to assess clear or collision situations as movement on the part of two objects is involved.

A useful exercise can be to cut out aircraft outlines from card or paper and with a protractor accurately mark out the respective lights – colouring them in when finished.

In moving the models about you will see for yourself the lights visible and their bearings in relation to whether a potential collision situation exists or not. A useful tip is this: if there is no change in the bearing of another aircraft then a potential collision situation exists.

If any required light should fail in flight the aircraft must land as soon as it is safe to do so unless authorised to continue by ATC.

A glider does not necessarily have to display full navigational lights as just discussed. It has the option to do as free balloons do and that is to display a steady red light visible in all directions.

An anti-collision light when carried on any aircraft is a flashing red light showing in all directions.

Air Light Beacons

Air light beacons are installed at various civil and military aerodromes in the UK. They come in two forms.

Identification beacons – These flash a two-letter Morse group every 12 seconds. Green at civil aerodromes Red at military aerodromes

Aerodrome beacons – An alternating colour flash signal usually white/green

Beacons normally operate at night and during the day if the visibility is bad.

Restrictions and Hazards in Airspace

There are areas over which flight may be restricted or prohibited either temporarily or permanently.

These areas are to be found outlined on aviation charts together with their vertical extent.

For example: D.308/25 on a chart indicates 'Danger area No.308' up to 25,000 ft within the area outlined. Also, the manner in which it is outlined will give an indication of times of operation.

Obstructions are shown when they are 300 feet and over; an example is a TV mast or similar form of obstruction reaching up to an abnormal height in relation to its environment. Such structures are lit if 500 ft or more above ground level (AGL). Between 300 and 500 ft AGL they may be lit. Such an obstruction will be designated by a specified symbol with two sets of figures – one is the height above ground level (QFE), the other is the height above sea level (QNH).

Always take care that you read these heights in accordance with your situation at the time – the difference can be quite substantial and therefore potentially hazardous.

Aeronautical Charts

To the light aeroplane or microlight pilot knowledge of the forms of airspace – particularly that which is controlled – is to know when to keep away!

Your best guide is the standard ICAO half million aeronautical chart which not only highlights the 'no-go' areas but the 'Reference to Air Information' section at the foot of the chart will teach you a great deal about the types of airspace we have discussed.

Such a chart should be definitely part of your reading alongside this book.

From time to time chart data can change. For operational use always ensure that you have an up-date issue.

Re-prints take place approximately every twelve months but changes can occur in between so reference should be made to **Aeronautical Information Service Publications**.

Aeronautical Information Service Publications

The UK Aeronautical Information Publication (UK AIP) – sometimes called the UK Air Pilot

Notams – sent by teleprinter only

Aeronautical Information Circulars (AICs) are:
- circulars which originate from the CAA monthly
- details of chart changes when printed on green paper
- concerned with flight safety when they are printed on pink paper.

Aerodrome Traffic Services

Air Traffic Control (ATC) is responsible for the control of all aircraft in the vicinity of the aerodrome and in the manoeuvring area. From a radio point of view a pilot starting up and taking off contacts the aerodrome 'tower' frequency. The pilot inward bound would first use the aerodrome 'approach' frequency and would be handed over to the 'tower' as and when it is thought to be appropriate.

Aerodrome Flight Information Service (AFIS) is provided when a no ATC is available. This service cannot give instructions or advice at any time and the suffix 'information' is used in any transmissions.

Air/Ground Radio Station facilities can exist where no ATC or AFIS is available and such stations may be manned by people without ATC qualifications. To make it clear that no ATC or AFIS are available the suffix 'radio' is used in any transmissions.

Radar Advisory Service

The **Radar Advisory Service** (RAS) provides separation advice to aircraft within the vicinity of each other and continuously suggests action to avoid traffic confliction until the possibility of such confliction ceases. The service will only be provided to flights under IFR.

In IMC a pilot is expected to accept the advice given. However, a pilot without an IMC rating should only do so if it enables VMC to be maintained and the controller should be informed if the situation is otherwise.

The pilot must inform the controller of any change in heading or level.

Should a pilot decide not to accept RAS advice, the controller must be informed and the pilot then takes all responsibility for any avoiding action. Unless the controller is told otherwise it will be assumed that a pilot is complying with advice given.

Radar Information Service

As with the RAS the pilot must inform the controller of any change in heading or level.

Documents carried in Flight

Should you travel overseas outside the UK – other than the Channel Islands or the Isle of Man – you must carry the following documents:
– The licence for any radio installation you may have on board.
– The aircraft's C of A or relevant airworthiness document.
– Your pilot's licence.
– Copy of Interception Procedures.
– The aircraft's registration certificate.
Again, do check your airworthiness document in relation to the aircraft being permitted to operate outside the UK.

Production of Documents

An authorised person such as a police constable, a CAA enforcement officer or any other person designated by the Secretary of State can ask you to produce documents.
These documents are
– Your pilot's licence
– Your personal flying log book
– The aircraft's registration certificate
– The aircraft's airworthiness documentation
Note:
Your personal flying log book must be kept by you for production when asked up to two years after the date of the last entry in any book.

Flying at Displays

Procedures for participating in flying displays are laid down in CAA Publication CAP 403. It is important to remember that if you are to perform at a display where more than 500 people are expected to attend then you will need to be in possession of a Display Pilot Authorisation issued by the CAA.

Displays held at Ministry of Defence establishments do not come under CAP 403 procedures but the organisers of flying displays at such locations will invariably require evidence of pilot competence such as a Display Pilot Authorisation issued by the CAA.

Rallies, competitions and races are not considered to be displays and do not come under the regulations laid down for displays; neither does the simple act of flying into and out of a display as a visitor.
Note: Dispensation from the 500 ft Low Flying Rule must be obtained from the CAA in respect of events other than major air displays.
Once again there are differences where the microlight is concerned.

Where **more than 500 people** are expected to be present, the pilot of a microlight aeroplane flying under a Type Approved Permit to Fly may take part in a public display but he or she must be in possession of a current Display Pilot Authorisation issued by the CAA. The flight limitations imposed by the Permit to Fly must not be exceeded.

In the case of a Type Accepted aeroplane flying in such a display, a dispensation is required from the CAA in respect of its airworthiness status.

Where **less than 500 people** are expected to be present at an event, such as a local fete or show, **no** Display Pilot Authorisation is required but the participant is strongly advised to discuss the matter with the CAA for the purposes of obtaining advice.

At an event organised by the BMAA or a club event conforming to the BMAA rules referred to below where **less than 500 people** are expected to be present at the flying part of the event, all microlight aeroplanes may participate provided the event is organised in accordance with conditions laid down in BMAA Document DP/2 as agreed with the CAA.

Flight limitations under BMAA DP/2 are as follows.

Degrees of Bank   60
Degrees of Pitch Up/Down   30
Intentional Stalling   Forbidden

Note: Manoeuvres must be less than above if so stated in handling notes.

Again, note: Dispensation from the 500 ft Low Flying Rule must be obtained from the CAA in respect of events other than major air displays.

Before accepting an invitation or seeking to take part in any public event, you should contact the CAA to see where you stand. The address is – Civil Aviation Authority, General Aviation Dept., Aviation House, South Area, Gatwick Airport, West Sussex RH6 0YR and the telephone number is 01293 567171 – Ask for General Aviation Dept.

Notifiable Accidents

An accident must be notified if it is a serious accident and happens from the time anyone, pilot or passengers, board an aircraft with the intention of flying until such time as everybody has left that aircraft.

By serious accident is meant:

– Anyone killed or seriously injured whilst in the aircraft or in direct contact with it.

or

– The aircraft suffers damage or structural failure which can affect its structural strength, performance or flight characteristics to the extent it needs major repairs.

or

– The aircraft is missing or completely inaccessible.

Note:
Exceptions to damage are engine failure or engine accessories and are limited to these alone.
– Also excepted is damage to propellers, wing tips, tyres, brakes, fairings or small dents and punctures to skin.
When a notifiable accident occurs, the aircraft commander **Pilot-in-Command (PIC)**, must notify the Chief Inspector of the Department of Transport, Air Accident Investigation Branch (AAIB) by the quickest possible means. Where the PIC is not in a position to do so, the report should be made by any other responsible person.

If the notifiable accident occurs in the UK the local police authority must also be notified.

All accidents/incidents, **however small,** must be entered up in the aeroplane's engine and airframe log book/s before the aeroplane is flown again or before the end of the day – whichever is the earlier.

Airmiss Reporting Procedure

If you consider that you have been endangered by the close proximity of another aircraft, you should radio a report at once to the nearest Air Traffic Service Unit.

If this is not possible the report should be made by telephone or any other means to any ATSU or preferably to the Air Traffic Control Centre immediately on landing. All reports, however made should be confirmed within 7 days on the appropriate CAA form.

Dropping of Articles from the Air

Other than the dropping of glider tow ropes and banners at permitted sites, no person or article may be dropped from an aircraft without prior permission from the CAA.

Registration of Aircraft

All aircraft in the UK with the exception of gliders and hang gliders must be registered with the CAA.

Registration letters of a stated size must be painted or affixed to the wings and fuselage of the aircraft.

The CAA must be notified of any change of ownership or additional ownership that takes place on an aircraft. To the Authority, it is the name which appears in the UK Register that they consider to be the person responsible even if that person has disposed of the aircraft.

Incidents

The good pilot never stops learning and one of the finest ways to do so is by one's own mistakes and those of others.

Within the flying world there are organisations which collect and publish anonymously reports of incidents which are not necessarily serious accidents but from which others can learn to avoid similar situations.

For example, an aeroplane owner on pre-flighting his machine may discover a hair-line crack in the structure. Memories sneak back of a previous heavy landing which 'fortunately' no one else had seen. Pride overwhelms conscience and the part is replaced with no report ever being made of the incident.

Suppose an identical situation had happened to other pilots? If each had submitted an incident report, a pattern would have emerged and a warning issued to owners of similar aeroplanes as to what could happen.

In doing so it is in no way trite to say that a life may be saved. Reading an accident report later and being able to say – 'that fault happened on my machine but I kept quiet' would not be a pleasant situation to live with.

Many incidents may not be reportable to the appropriate authorities but they are certainly bound to be reported in the aircraft's engine/air-frame log book to alert the inspector. In fact if the aeroplane is not immediately and safely flyable it must be grounded and any repairs officially inspected and passed as satisfactory before further flight can take place.

Do remember, incident reports are anonymous when passed on to others, so help those others. Not to do so is the mark of a very irresponsible pilot.

Alcohol

There must be eight clear hours between the consumption of even the smallest amount of alcohol and your piloting an aeroplane.

It is illegal for *anyone*, not just the crew, to board an aircraft when drunk.

Commercial Use of Microlights

The commercial use of any aeroplane for hire and reward, where money or goods in kind change hands for services rendered, is strictly speaking only allowed when the pilot has a Commercial Pilot's Licence (CPL).

Currently there is no microlight CPL in existence, so you are unable to undertake any flying which can be termed commercial. There is however a dispensation in that a microlight pilot with an Instructor Rating in his/her licence can be paid for their services, but only for the purposes of flight training in respect of a pilot's licence.

But the instructor and the student concerned must be members of the same club and the microlight used for instructional purposes must be owned or operated under arrangements entered into with that club.

Furthermore, the aeroplane used for such training must be Type Approved except in special circumstances. Although complicated, without this dispensation microlight flying could well have disappeared.

Other Aspects of Hire and Reward

The law is quite complex and other areas are involved which because money can change hands the activities are deemed to be commercial – or illegal because the aeroplane does not meet a required airworthiness standard.

Other than for the purposes of flight training towards attaining your licence you cannot hire a microlight, because such hire can only be undertaken when the aeroplane holds a Certificate of Airworthiness in the Public Transport Category. Quite simply, this means that a microlight pilot has to buy his/her own aeroplane or enter into a syndicate after obtaining a licence.

Even here the situation is not straightforward. The *solitary owner* of an aeroplane may pay an instructor for flight tuition – even if the aeroplane is not Type Approved. But, where there is *multiple ownership*, such as in a syndicate where money has already changed hands in the sharing of costs, no further money may change hands for other purposes such as flight instruction.

Again, not so long ago, it was illegal to share the costs of flying in that a passenger could not contribute towards the expenses incurred by the flight where the pilot did not hold a CPL. This has now been relaxed and a private pilot may accept a contribution towards costs where the amount is not more than an equal share contributed by all on board the aircraft – *including the pilot*. So, in a microlight the maximum contribution would be 50%.

Charity Flights

This is one sphere of activity which has become very popular in recent years.

Money may be raised for charities in a microlight aeroplane or powered parachute provided that a pilot flying a sponsored flight receives no payment for that flight.

No passenger may be carried in a microlight aeroplane on a sponsored charity flight or in respect of a prize for partaking in such as a raffle or other form of fund raising activity. A microlight aeroplane flies on a Permit to Fly whereas the carriage of passengers on such occasions requires that an aircraft has a full Certificate of Airworthiness in the Public Transport category.

The Other Side

And so we come to the end of our journey through the complexities of air law as far as the microlight pilot and aeroplane are concerned.

However, you may well meet up with pilots flying a different category of aircraft to that which you fly yourself and they may also hold one of those additional ratings referred to earlier.

In these circumstances the situation may arise that a statement you make on air law will be disputed by such pilots, so we will round off with a few sections of the law that can apply to them. On this occasion you can relax as you will be reading only from an interest point of view as the * and ** denote.

Flight Conditions/Rules

Flight within the United Kingdom comes under two sets of defined flight weather conditions and flight rules according to the nature of the airspace in which the flight is being made.

The flight weather conditions are

Visual Meteorological Conditions (VMC).

When they fall *below* this minima they are known as

Instrument Meteorological Conditions (IMC).

The flight rules are

Visual Flight Rules   **(VFR)**
Instrument Flight Rules   **(IFR)**

At certain times operating within them can require that you have a Rating *additional* to your basic PPL.

Ratings

Instrument Meteorological Conditions (IMC) Rating

The IMC Rating allows a pilot to fly as PIC
- out of sight of the surface or in cloud
- on a Special VFR flight in visibility down to three kilometres – but not less
- on take-off and/or landing in visibility below cloud down to not less than 1800 metres.

Night Rating

A Night Rating entitles a pilot to be PIC of an aircraft flying at night provided such rating is kept current by the completion of five take-offs and landings at night within the previous thirteen months.

Instrument Rating (IR)

The Instrument Rating entitles a pilot to be PIC of an aircraft flying in certain controlled airspace which requires compliance with IFR (Instrument Flight Rules).

Visual Flight Rules (VFR)

Outside Controlled Airspace – within Class F and G airspace

Visual Flight Rules (VFR) state that an aircraft, other than a helicopter, may fly subject to the VMC minima laid out below.

Note: In the criteria that follows *each* stated limitation of visibility and horizontal/vertical separation from cloud requires compliance at the same time during any part of the flight.

(a) Above Flight Level (FL) 100 there is no speed limitation but the aircraft must remain
   – with an in-flight visibility of at least eight kilometres
   – at least 1500 metres horizontally from cloud
   – at least 1000 feet vertically from cloud

(b) At or below Flight Level (FL) 100 there is a speed limitation of 250 knots and the aircraft must remain
   – with an in-flight visibility of at least five kilometres
   – at least 1500 metres horizontally from cloud
   – at least 1000 feet vertically from cloud
        or alternatively

In the UK

In the UK, an aircraft may fly with a speed not exceeding 250 knots at or below 3000 feet AMSL but it must remain
   – with an in-flight visibility of at least five kilometres
   – clear of cloud
   – in sight of the surface
        however

Below 3000 feet, with a speed not exceeding 140 knots IAS, the limitations are as per the second alternative in (b) above except for the in-flight visibility limitation which is reduced to 1500 metres.

Do remember that the alternatives within (b) apply within the UK only although it is possible that some other states may have adopted them. If you intend to fly abroad you should check to see if the country concerned operates under these or any other agreed alternatives.

To fly within the privileges of the Private Pilots Licence (Aeroplanes), in accordance with the above VMC minima, requires that you hold an IMC or Instrument Rating.

Inside Controlled Airspace   **– Within Class A Airspace – VFR not applicable**

          – Within Class B, D, and E Airspace – as follows

An aircraft may still fly under VFR by day when it can conform with the following VMC minima

– above FL100; have an in-flight visibility of at least eight kilometres
    or
– below FL100; have an in-flight visibility of at least five kilometres
    and in both cases
– be at least 1500 metres horizontally and 1000 feet vertically from cloud
  – except in Class B airspace where it need only remain clear of cloud
– fly at a speed not exceeding 250 knots IAS below FL100 – except in Class B airspace where the speed restriction does not apply
– have obtained ATC clearance in Class B and D airspace

Note: – Special VFR clearance may be obtainable from ATC for flight in a Control Zone (CTR).

    – An exemption exists in the UK only which permits flight by aircraft in Class D, E and C (when allocated) airspace at or below 3000 feet AMSL at a speed of 140 knots or less which remains clear of cloud and an in-flight visibility of at least 5km.

Instrument Flight Rules (IFR)/Altimeter Settings

For newcomers to flying, discussing IFR requires only a brief insight. Instrument Flight Rules apply when weather conditions become IMC unless a Special VFR is granted, or flight takes place in Class A controlled airspace, or the pilot elects to fly IFR.

Outside Controlled Airspace – within Class F and G airspace

(a) Subject to low flying requirements the aircraft may not fly at less than 1000 feet above the highest obstacle within 5 nm.

Exceptions to the rule are
– taking off and landing
– when flying at or below 3000 feet AMSL, clear of cloud and in sight of the surface
– when on a route authorised by ATC

(b) At or below 3000 feet AMSL or below transition altitude a pilot may use any altimeter setting but beneath a TMA or CTA the QNH of an aerodrome beneath that area should be used.

(c) Above 3000 feet AMSL, or transition altitude if it is higher, unless directed by ATC, a pilot will select a cruising level based on the altimeter set at the Standard Pressure Setting of 1013.2 mb and will express any vertical position report as a Flight Level (FL).

The flight level selected under the rules in (c) will be related to the aircraft's magnetic track in compliance with **Quadrantal** or **Semi Circular Height Rules** as follows:

Quadrantal – below FL245 (24,500 feet)

Magnetic Track	Cruising Level
Less than 090 degrees	Odd thousands of feet
090 but less than 180 degrees	Odd thousands of feet + 500 feet
180 but less than 270 degrees	Even thousands of feet
270 but less than 360 degrees	Even thousands of feet + 500 feet

Semi-Circular – above FL245

Magnetic Track	Cruising Level
Less than 180 degrees	25,000 feet (lowest usable)
	27,000 feet
	29,000 feet
	At higher levels
	4000 feet intervals
180 but less than 360 degrees	26,000 feet (lowest usable)
	28,000 feet
	31,000 feet
	At higher levels
	4000 feet intervals

Inside Controlled Airspace – within Class A, B, D and E Airspace

(a) The same as (a) under 'Outside Controlled Airspace'

(b) A flight plan must be lodged and ATC clearance obtained. The flight plan must be adhered to unless instructed otherwise by ATC.

(c) Any switch from IFR to VFR can only be made if the flight can continue in uninterrupted VMC whilst in controlled airspace and ATC are informed that the flight plan is cancelled. This does not apply if the airspace is designated for IFR only (Class A).

(d) Unless a flight plan is cancelled an aircraft commander must inform ATC on landing or leaving controlled airspace.

(e) An aircraft flying under IFR which is in, or intends to enter, controlled airspace must report time, position and flight level at such intervals and reporting points as directed by ATC. **

Foot Launched Powered Flying Machine (FLPFM)

Introduction

FLPFMs should not be confused with powered parachutes which have been flying for some years and are composed of a canopy and a trike unit. The FLPFM is classified as a microlight but by virtue of being foot launchable and its overall limited performance, it does not have to meet with airworthiness, registration and pilot licensing requirements, under a General Exemption from the Air Navigation Order (ANO).

Currently, FLPFMs are composed of paragliders with the power unit strapped to the pilot's back. However, also included in the FLPFM category are hang-gliders to which an engine has been attached to make them self-sustaining in the air. Again they must be capable of being foot launched.

Definition

For the purposes of this *(the CAA)* General Exemption, a Foot Launched Powered Flying Machine is defined as a powered flying machine which:

- comprises a combination of a parachute or flexwing aerofoil and a mechanical propulsion device
- is demonstrably capable of being safely foot launched from a horizontal surface in still air or light wind conditions
- is capable of carrying no more than two persons in flight
- has a maximum fuel capacity of 10 litres
- has a maximum unladen weight, including full fuel, of 60 kg for single-place aircraft and 70 kg for two-place aircraft.

Operation

Broadly speaking, in flight the pilot is subject to the same rules of the air as the microlight pilot; the words General Exemption in no way imply total freedom.

Operating Conditions

1   The pilot should be aged 16 years or over.
2   The aircraft should be foot launched.
3   The aircraft should not be flown:
   – other than for private purposes
   – by night
   – other than in sight of the surface and subject to the flight visibility and cloud clearance requirements given in The table in Fig.1

Fig 1
Flight Visibility and Cloud Clearance

Airspace	Flight Visibility	Distance from Cloud
Class A to E Controlled Airspace	Flight prohibited	Flight prohibited
Class F and G Open Airspace	Above Flight Level 100 (Approximately 10,000 ft)	
	8 km	1000 ft vertically and 1500 m horizontally
	At or below Flight Level 100 (approx 10,000 ft) but below 3000 ft AMSL	
	5 km	1000 ft vertically and 1500 m horizontally
	At or below 3000 ft AMSL	
	3 km	Clear of cloud

Note: The present mixture of metric and imperial measure (metres and feet) is accepted by international convention.

   – over any congested area of a city, town or settlement
   – closer than 500 ft to any person, vessel, building or structure except while it is landing in accordance with normal aviation practice or while hill soaring with the engine stopped
   – during take-off within 500 ft of a structure (which the pilot could reasonably expect to be inhabited) unless the structure is either the

property of the pilot or prior permission has been obtained from the occupiers
- when towing any article (including any glider)
- within any Aerodrome Traffic Zone unless with the permission of the appropriate Air Traffic Control Unit
- within Controlled Airspace
- within any Prohibited, Danger or Restricted Area.

4 No person shall cause or permit an article or person to be dropped from the aircraft.

5 Notwithstanding RULE 17 *(of the ANO)*, such aircraft should yield right of way to all other aircraft. In the event of two such aircraft converging, the aircraft which has the other on its right should give way; further, if approaching head-on or approximately so and there is danger of collision, each should alter course to the right.

Although no licence is required and therefore no examinations have to be taken, the BMAA and the BHPA have initiated simple test papers linked to the rules of the air to which they will have to comply. In fact, it should be stressed that, in spite of the absence of the need for a licence, anyone attempting to fly a powered parachute without expert tuition would be very foolish.

As all FLPFM pilots will be accountable under the conditions laid down by law, the responsible ones will naturally seek the guidance both associations are prepared to offer.

The need is not only a knowledge of Air Law to keep on the right side of the law but also a need to digest the various aspects of aviation as covered in this book for the sake of flight safety alone.

Human Performance Limitations

Introduction

The relatively slow speed and low operating altitudes of the normal microlight aeroplane may lead the student pilot to consider the subject of Human Performance Limitations (HPL) to be unnecessary. This is not so; we are all human and according to our state of health in general or at a particular moment there are factors which can affect our ability to fly safely and accurately. Certainly there are some aspects of the subject which can be immediately irrelevant but with the future in mind there can come a time when such knowledge is crucial. The student microlight pilot of today may well be the microlight pilot who attempts an altitude record at some time in the future and with the 'experience' gained by then there may be an apathy towards further study.

In this section every endeavour has been made to keep the subject relevant to the microlight aeroplane with its operating limitations in mind and the constraints under which it flies. Where the requirements of a medical may be touched upon they are worth noting even though they may not strictly speaking apply to the microlight pilot flying on a Declaration of Fitness.

Human Requirement for Oxygen

That a human being must have oxygen to live is a statement of the obvious; but it is important when flying to understand where it may not be present in sufficient quantity to ensure you have adequate control of your actions.

The atmosphere to all intents and purposes is composed of 21% oxygen to 78% nitrogen; the other 1% being composed of carbon dioxide, water vapour, argon and so forth. In the section on meteorology the relationship of pressure, temperature and density are discussed and this has a bearing on the amount of oxygen your body can receive as you climb above the surface of the Earth.

To the fit person the effect of a lack of oxygen, known as *hypoxia*, will not normally make itself felt below 10,000 feet; however it can start to tell at 8000 feet if you are perhaps below par. At this lower height it is the ability to learn to take in something new that can be affected rather than the ability to practice previously acquired skills. Over 10,000 feet you must be aware of potential problems. The picture is thus.

Ground – 10,000 feet

An intake of normal air is sufficient except where, as previously stated, a learning process is involved.

10,000 – 33,700 feet

Oxygen must be added to the air inhaled.

33,700 – 40,000 feet

It is necessary to breath 100% oxygen.

Above 40,000 feet

100% oxygen must be taken in under pressure as air pressure is insufficient to force the gas into the body.

From your study of meteorology you will be aware that the higher you go, the more rarified becomes the air. The percentage of oxygen in the atmosphere remains the same but there is less of it. Also, the pressure is steadily reducing until there comes a time when it is insufficient to 'push' the gas into your lungs. It is then that it must be induced under pressure.

To keep the environment as near to sea level as possible, cabins of commercial and other high flying aeroplanes are pressurised. Thus an aircraft at 35,000 feet will have a cabin pressure equivalent to flying at below 10,000 feet.

Hypoxia

As the brain is the most susceptible part of the body to lack of oxygen it is one's judgement that will be first to suffer through hypoxia. At 20,000 feet the onset can be slow but at 30,000 feet the effects can be so quick as to be unnoticed. Symptoms can be the lips and fingertips turning blue.
The effects of hypoxia can be as follows.

- judgement becomes sloppy with a pilot unawareness that performance is lacking. Also, decisions are made at a slower speed and co-ordination of movements are less smooth as muscles become affected.
- the senses of touch, vision and hearing all begin to be affected.
- there can be a personality change where one's outlook ranges from a slap-happy approach to one of aggression.
- all the time consciousness is dropping away and death can result at high altitude if an oxygen supply is not restored in time.

This leads to discussing some of the ways in which the effects of hypoxia can be accelerated.

- smoking produces carbon monoxide which impedes the passage of oxygen to essential parts of the body. This factor is obviously avoidable by choice.

- the longer the time of exposure and the greater the altitude are naturally two ways which will speed up the effect.
- the energy demands of the body if greater than normal; for example crew members exercising themselves in physical activity about the aeroplane as opposed to those sitting down will be affected more quickly. Likewise a person who is unwell will be subject to greater energy demands in the combating of the illness. Again, cold makes greater energy demands on the body.
- the presence of alcohol in the body.

Hyperventilation

Over-breathing is technically known as *hyperventilation*. It is associated with exhaling or 'ventilating' more carbon dioxide than is necessary in the normal breathing process; it is not confined directly to a lack of oxygen as a basic cause. In fact it can be argued that there can be occasions when the oxygen balance can be too high if too much carbon dioxide is expelled from the lungs. Hyperventilation can happen on the surface as well as at an altitude.

The effort to take in more oxygen can lead to over-breathing but hypoxia is not the only factor that can lead to this condition. It can be caused amongst other things by anxiety, air sickness, heat and vibration.

Taking anxiety in particular; it has just been named as a cause of hyperventilation but the situation can worsen as the anxiety of needing to breathe faster leads to further anxiety resulting in a potential vicious circle. Signs of this problem are tingling at extremities of the body such as hands, feet, lips and there can be hot/cold feelings anywhere on the body. Pilot performance drops off and vision can become tunnelled or clouded.

Where confusion occurs in flight as to whether a pilot may be suffering from hypoxia or hyperventilation, the problem should be treated as hypoxia unless below 10,000 feet where a determined effort must be made to regulate the over-breathing. In so doing normal breathing will be restored.

Barotrauma

As one ascends the atmospheric pressure drops and as it does so any pocket of air trapped within the body will end up at a higher pressure than the air outside. If this air cannot escape to equalise with the outside air to restore equilibrium then *barotrauma* is said to exist and it can create problems. This is particularly so where the ears and sinuses are concerned which can become blocked during colds or flu. Pilots with such ailments must not fly; doing so could eventually render them unfit to fly for many weeks.

A pilot should pay particular attention to the possibility of barotrauma in passengers during descent from altitude. Briefing them to swallow hard, or better still, hold the nose and blow hard with the mouth closed is to be highly recommended. If the ears do not clear it may be necessary to climb back up to reappraise the situation. Certainly the tips given should be started early in the descent and repeated at intervals; they should not be left until the last minute.

Within the body itself gases can build up through eating rich or spicy types of food and drinking beer. If the gases so produced cannot escape through the normal channels of mouth or rear then considerable pain and even fainting can result. If you are going to fly high – watch your diet.

Common Ailments

Following on from the ailments discussed under 'Barotrauma', apart from colds and flu, a pilot is unfit to fly when suffering from such ailments as diarrhoea, nausea, vomiting. There is every reason not to fly when taking medication whether purchased by oneself or prescribed by the doctor. They will often have side effects which will impair the ability to fly safely. When in doubt, clearance from an aviation doctor should be sought.

Decompression

People who take up flying may be termed adventurous types and therefore likely to take part in other forms of exhilarating sports, for example scuba diving.

Breathing in this activity is by means of compressed air and without delving into the technicalities you should not fly within 12 hours of swimming by these means and you must wait 24 hours if you have been below 30 feet under water.

Air Sickness

This form of sickness, also referred to as motion sickness, is said to stem from the motion one undergoes as opposed to the motion one is expecting. It is capable of being overcome by becoming adapted rather than by medication which can hamper the flight performance of a pilot. If you do take medication then consult an aviation doctor as some forms of treatment are not suitable for the pilot of an aeroplane.

A form of sickness experienced in the air not related to the above may well be due to a first flight and the tension attached thereto; also a hot stuffy environment can be another cause. A pilot should pay particular care to passenger comfort and should terminate the flight if necessary rather than put a companion off flying for good.

Hearing

Noise is measured in a unit known as the decibel. We live in a noisy world and short-term exposure to loud noise can cause a temporary loss of hearing. Should exposure to a source of this nature be long-term then permanent deafness or loss of hearing can result. Such noise would be around 90 decibels and over.

The length of time that one is exposed to noise is not the only factor; there is the level to be considered as well. For example an increase of only 30% in a noise level of 90 decibels will do the same amount of damage in 1 minute that the 90 decibels would do in 8 hours.

If you attend discos or indulge in listening to high volume stereo you are making a choice as to your exposure. If you work in a job or indulge in pastimes where there is a high element of noise attached, you would be well advised to consider ear plugs or defenders. Flying a microlight can be deemed to be in such a category. Use of radio need not be precluded by the addition of some form of protection for the ears.

Sight

Defect in sight does not pose a problem to a pilot as long as the defect can be corrected with spectacles or contact lenses. The medical requirement would expect a car number plate to be read at around 40 metres – a similar but stiffer requirement than the 23 metres required for driving a car.

Bifocals are the answer to those who need correction for both long and short sightedness. If you are in any doubt you should contact an aviation medical examiner.

Care should be taken in the use of certain types of sunglasses which vary with the intensity of light. The delay in change from one format to another could cause a problem.

The use of sight in the air is covered in more detail later when the avoidance of aerial collisions is discussed.

Toxic Hazards

Although the microlight is basically a very open air form of flying with the engine more often than not placed to the rear of the pilot, there are some types which are quite sophisticated with cabins appearing on the scene and a tractor type format with the engine in front. The possibility of unwanted exhaust fumes must be considered – particularly when some ingenious form of 'cabin heating' may be considered as an offshoot from the exhaust system.

Carbon monoxide emitted from exhaust is colourless and has no smell but it can bring on headaches, breathlessness and eventually render one unconscious.

You may recall that hypoxia can be accelerated by smoking. The intake of over 20 cigarettes per day can create a situation where your reactions will be influenced by an induced oxygen related environment which will be the equivalent of 3–4000 feet above your actual altitude. Again, this is an avoidable factor by choice.

Vapour from fuel and lubricants can make one drowsy when inhaled.

Blood Pressure

Treatment for blood pressure subsequent to regular monitoring need not preclude a pilot flying after the necessary checks have been carried out.

Epilepsy

Although not strictly a disease, epilepsy is unfortunately associated, to a lesser or greater degree according to circumstances, with a distinct loss of consciousness and therefore a pilot's licence would not be granted even when such attacks are deemed to be sufficiently under control to permit driving a car.

Alcohol/Drugs

The consumption of even the smallest amount of alcohol within 8 hours of flying is certainly not recommended. The pilot who becomes alcoholic must seek treatment and can resume flying after same, although total abstinence would be essential from then on. Even when an alcohol dependency may not exist, the level of intake can still be damaging. Taking a 'unit' of alcohol to be half a pint of beer or a normal glass of wine, medical opinions consider that above the range 21 to 28 units for a man and 14 to 21 units for a woman per week can be damaging. When flying you should adhere to the lower figure.

It should be remembered that it takes the body at least 1 hour to dispose of 1 unit of alcohol.

Concerning drugs those which can have an effect on the brain, and are taken say for depression or neurosis, preclude any flying as pilot/crew whilst being taken. A pilot wishing to resume flying would need to show a current record of good health and freedom from the drugs before being permitted to do so.

If intending to fly, seek authoritative medical advice when taking any form of drug; even a common cold treatment can contain antihistamines.

'Soft' drugs, as they can be termed, which are illegal cannot be entertained where flying is concerned due to the very nature of their effect.

Knowledge and the Senses

Just like driving a car, the pilot of an aeroplane makes decisions which result from assessing what is seen, heard, felt and even smelt followed by action in accordance with present knowledge previously gained. There are occasions when this sequence can incorporate several actions taking place at the same time. The degree to which this happens will depend on the depth of knowledge and the length of time such knowledge has been put into practice, namely experience.

When talking of 'experience' it is as well to understand that effective experience is based on accurate knowledge. In all walks of life one can meet people who will utter such words as 'I have 20 years experience'. This can be a dangerous state of mind. It can shut out an awareness that there is always something new to be learned but in many cases where acquired knowledge has been faulty, it can be a case of possibly 1 year of experience followed by 19 years of perpetuating error!

Knowledge can be termed the fundamental requirement but faults in the senses can lead to a misuse of knowledge in the making of wrong decisions. Consider the short-sighted pilot who may not spot a potential collision course or the pilot with a hearing problem which may lead to a failure or misinterpretation of an instruction given in the air or received from the ground.

Speed of perception and action can be affected by age. Forgetting experience for a moment, a pilot under 30 years of age will normally react more swiftly than one who is over 60.

Again, being ready for a decision-making situation leads to a much faster response. The microlight pilot who flies with a potential landing ground in mind in case of an engine failure will not be caught out should the power suddenly fail. Furthermore, the reactions will be smoother and safer as a result. The pilot who is not prepared for a situation will take longer to respond.

Attention to detail during flight can be less during an easy period, such a leisurely cruise, compared with the attention that is sharpened up during a landing. Watch this point because the last thing one wants is a casual attitude when the potential of a mid-air collision is in the making during a more relaxed part of the flight.

One final point on sharpening up one's wits when the need arises. Airspeed on approach can be termed a critical factor but it will serve no useful purpose if all effort is geared up to watching the ASI; one may miss the aircraft that has just cut in ahead and below. There has to be an awareness of the need to look almost virtually in two places at once.

Knowledge and perception need to be good and they rely on a healthy mind and body. However, even these factors alone are not necessarily enough as they can easily be impaired by the bad cockpit environment or poorly laid out controls and instrument panel found in some aircraft; for example the rear seat of a flexwing microlight is a less easy pilot position than the front seat.

Disorientation

One does not have to be involved in flying for very long before hearing of the horrendous results that can come about by flying in cloud without the necessary instruments and training. The microlight pilot is forbidden to enter cloud but, without going into detail, should the temptation arise be sure that all control of the aircraft could be lost within a very short space of time.

Sight is no longer available to help the untrained pilot in an ill-equipped aeroplane and the other senses will quickly begin to mislead the 'intrepid' (?) aviator. Feelings will enter the picture, which will be totally divorced from what is actually happening and any reactions based on such feelings will accelerate a situation from which recovery may be unlikely.

Do not be tempted into cloud however innocent it may seem.

Avoiding the Airmiss

The avoidance of potential collisions is drummed into a pilot from the outset. 'Look-out' is given a high priority in training and a pupil pilot who flies faultlessly but fails in this aspect will surely not pass a General Flying Test.

There is a potential for collision when two aeroplanes are close to each other in the air or even at a distance given certain factors are present.

Unless in a pre-arranged formation situation the behaviour of a nearby aircraft who is unaware of your presence is unpredictable. Should it be at the same altitude, a sudden change of heading on the part of the pilot who is ignorant of your presence has all the makings of a problem. So if for one reason or another you are going to be in close proximity to another aircraft, take steps to ensure your presence is known.

Avoidance of a collision where a distant aircraft can pose a threat requires not only an understanding of **what** is perceived but also **how** to perceive the situation in the first place – the latter being concerned with the behaviour of the human eye.

Whether an aircraft is flying straight and level, climbing or descending and at whatever speed and heading it may have adopted, there is a risk of a collision if one aircraft remains on a constant bearing in relation to the other.

You can identify this situation when you spot another aircraft which to all intents and purposes seems to be stationary in your vision with no movement across your cabin window or in relation to some other part of your machine if you happen to be sitting outside as is the case with most microlights.

The fact that it appears to be stationary makes it harder to notice in the first place. The only indication of a likely collision would be an awareness that it was growing larger in your vision but herein lies another problem. At the very high speeds at which the modern jet can travel the oncoming aircraft may not have grown large enough to be noticed until collision is unavoidable.

To give an instance of this speed problem. An aircraft flying at 600 kts towards another flying at 200 kts gives a closing speed of 800 kts. To the pilots maintaining 'look-out' each will appear as a mere dot within three seconds of an impact. There could be but a tenth of a second left when the aircraft is large enough to attract attention without its presence actually being sought after in a search.

A microlight may travel at a relatively slow speed of say 60 kts but a low flying military jet doing 500 kts still produces a closing speed of nearly 600 kts. For example, spotting a jet at 3 nm with a closing speed of 600 kts gives you less than 20 seconds before possible impact! A sighting at 5 nm and a closing speed of 500 kts still only gives you 30 to 40 seconds.

Should the jet be an aircraft such as a Tornado, then the wings could well be folded back and the image mass will be even less easy to spot. In the UK, where the recognized bands of height at which such a hazard can be met being advised as between surface and 500 feet AGL, the pilot has at least an opportunity to minimise the risk by keeping at 1000 feet AGL and above.

The resolution of this unpleasant prospect related to high speed aircraft lies in maintaining the best possible effective look-out and in so doing you may think you are viewing the whole sky at one time when continuously moving your eyes around. In fact when it comes to spotting such a minute dot as an oncoming aircraft, the **continuously** moving eye cannot cope.

To take in such detail the eye must be constantly moved to the various parts of the sky with a **pause** to take in the segment being searched at any given moment. Continuous movement of the eye will not achieve this aim.

If any part of the aircraft structure is in your line of vision this will call for head movement as well as eye movement. It takes very little to obscure the minute speck of a fast approaching jet.

Stress

The stress with which we are concerned is not the arousal of excitement or heightening of tension at a critical point in a flight such as landing or an emergency being handled by an experienced pilot under normal conditions.

The stress we shall discuss is that which can affect judgement rather than enhance it – the stress synonymous with present day living and it affects individuals in different ways. It can come from within a person by virtue of their make-up or it can be imposed from outside. There is of course a close link up between the two in the end result.

Taking that which can come from within, the pilot with a vivid imagination can undergo far more stress than the more phlegmatic one. The former may see and prepare for a host of problems which could arise but usually never do. Fear causes this form of stress and as fear stems from the unknown this situation can decline as the individual experiences problems and learns to cope. However, it is unlikely that such feelings will be eradicated totally because it is in the very 'nature of the beast' to feel that way.

The more phlegmatic pilot will not be so affected and consequently has a much less stressful flight. However, should an emergency occur the prepared pilot could be in a better position to cope due to the mental alertness already in place for a given situation – the more carefree one being left to think much more rapidly.

There is perhaps an element of truth in the saying that a pilot should always have a slight 'knot in the stomach' on take-off. It portrays an awareness and a respect for the air and the responsibility of taking an aircraft into that environment. One has only to consider the number of small boat rescue operations that take place off our coast when untrained 'sailors' (?) take to the water blissfully ignorant of the potential perils of the sea.

Undue stress of the wrong sort will cause problems in flying because it can affect or influence judgement and decision making – even to the extent of inducing panic in an emergency.

Let us look at some of the outside influences that can lead to stress in recreational flying.

Competing A pilot becomes caught up in trying to match others by flying in conditions within the capability of his companions but not within his/her own capability.

Deadline Being caught out by time – the get-home-at-all costs attitude despite deteriorating weather or the approach of nightfall. The number of pilots who have never made the deadline they saw as crucial is unfortunately very considerable.

Domestic Problems in the family can cause considerable stress and the pilot who leaves home to fly an aircraft in a state of temper after a family row, concern over an illness or even worse a bereavement, will not be in a fit state to think clearly. It is imperative that the illusion is not nurtured that going aloft will relax one or take one away from such problems. The stress will be there and judgement will be impaired.

Low hours The pilot who does not have the opportunity to fly frequently will be under much more stress than the one who is regularly in the air.

Fatigue It surely must go without saying that fatigue through over-work, lack of sleep or poor diet will inevitably induce stress. The pilot can become subject to a failure to respond to events with the necessary speed and accuracy. The situation will further deteriorate if common ailments or poor health in general are present.

The amount of sleep needed varies considerably with each person. The older one gets the less sleep one requires we are told. But, the older one gets the less becomes the choice of times of sleep. A young shift worker may take varying sleep times in his/her stride but the older person cannot cope so well.

Where insomnia is involved which can lead to fatigue, advice should be sought as any drugs prescribed must be approved and the nature of the cause of the problem iden-tified. Just as drugs for common ailments can temporarily preclude flying, the same applies to drugs for inducing sleep.

Noise Undue noise, and to this can be added vibration, will certainly be stress inducing. Attention should be paid to the reduction of such problem sources.

Temperature Excessive heat and excessive cold can cause discomfort and thereby lead to stress through an unsuitable environment.

Managing Stress

Easier said than done for some but there are ways in which stress can be reduced and controlled. The dangers of doing so by the use of unprescribed drugs or the absence of medical advice has already been discussed.

Talking over one's fears and problems with a close friend or colleague can help enormously. Although it may come as a surprise to some, such conversation can reveal that others have the same concern but do not appear to show it. From such a revelation can come consolation in not being alone but more importantly it can lead to learning how others have coped. Seeking professional counselling should not be ruled out.

Keeping fit provides a well-tuned healthy body which is much more able to cope with stress than one below par. Some pilots practise meditation and other such techniques. If a religious belief is present this may well help to control stress in the sense that the worries and concerns are looked at in a different context to the non-believer.

Experience and practice will definitely contribute to reducing stress – take the problem of the low-hours pilot mentioned earlier. It is well worth such a pilot swallowing pride and seeking regular check flights with an instructor. The most critical moment in flying is no doubt the landing. The pilot who builds up air time for the sake of keeping within the law is never going to have the confidence and thereby be as less stressed as the one who confines his limited flying to repeated practice of taking off and landing in the circuit.

Social Psychology

Social psychology deals with the inter-relationship of people one to another and is primarily important when one considers flight deck personnel in a large aeroplane being able to work together harmoniously.

In a microlight such a situation does not exist but there is one aspect of psychology that does need to be considered: it is probably the most powerful urge in the human make-up, namely the ego. Participation in many adventure sports is simply undertaken to satisfy this urge and there is nothing wrong in that. Learning new skills and facing new challenges is healthy and can change the outlook of a humble office clerk into one that sees a managerial post achieved which might never have been the case.

It is when the ego-trip gets out of hand that problems can arise. A pilot is trained to fly and the aeroplane is designed to fly; but both are limited in what their performance can be if safe flight is to take place. Curbing the ego calls for self-discipline.

Unfortunately there is a mistaken impression that throwing an aeroplane about the sky, usually exceeding laid down performance limitations, is the criteria by which a 'good' pilot is judged. Never could such an impression be so wrong.

Aerobatic manoeuvres require special pilot training and they also require special aircraft in which to perform them. The pilot not in possession of both these requirements who feels the urge to emulate the 'masters' is not a good pilot. In so doing a lack of self control is displayed which means an inability to handle the aircraft intelligently.

Certainly in the case of prototype test pilots there is a need for stretching the aeroplane to its limits, but those who do so will be found to be the most careful and meticulously disciplined pilots on this planet with no desire to impress or be flamboyant.

With the over-confident pilot for whom flying has no fears there is the danger of being unaware of performance limitations – that is the ability to undertake certain actions. In such cases there is a need for a conscious self-discipline to be imposed on oneself. The cure can sometimes be accelerated by an unpleasant experience which provides a short sharp lesson. At the risk of appearing critical of over-confidence it must be acknowledged that in a war-time situation the element of recklessness can pay off; but in recreational flying there is no place for such an approach.

Another aspect of self-discipline was referred to earlier in respect of the low-hour pilot not being reticent about seeking a check flight or refresher training.

Regrettably the result of a rebuttal of one's own Human Performance Limitations is often painful and irrevocable with the pilot becoming another statistic in the records.

For the very few who may not have heard the saying – take heed.

'There are old pilots and bold pilots,

But – there are no old, bold pilots.'

Meteorology

Wind Effect

Introduction

A jet airliner can plough through weather that a light aeroplane would find prohibitive. In turn, a light aeroplane or glider can take to the air when some microlights must remain on the ground. This makes meteorology particularly important to a microlight pilot.

Prior to discussing the subject in general, the initial pages of this chapter will cover an aspect you are certain to experience from the outset of your flight tuition; the marked effect of wind on a microlight aeroplane due to its relatively light weight.

Wind

Wind is nothing more than air moving from one place to another – a movement from an area of high pressure to an area of low pressure.

Take two tumblers – one full of water and the other empty. Join them with an imaginary tube at the base and both will end up holding equal amounts of water. (Fig.1)

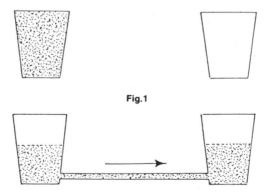

Fig.1

Air is a fluid and behaves as the water in the tumblers – flowing from high pressure to low pressure in order to establish equilibrium.

Other factors affect this simple analogy but they will be discussed later.

Let us examine the ways in which wind plays its part in microlight flying – for good or evil.

Wind Direction

The direction of wind is based on the point *from* which it is blowing. In terms of aviation this is expressed in degrees from 001° to 360°. (Fig.2)

Fig.2

Windspeed

We have to face a snag at the outset. Wind speed in both meteorological and aviation terms is expressed in nautical miles per hour – knots. When requesting official wind information you will receive it in degrees/knots; for example 240/15.

It so happens that many microlights still continue to come with airspeed indicators (ASIs) calibrated in statute miles per hour – mph. This leaves you with a small calculation to make. A nautical mile is equal to one and one seventh statute miles so a reported wind of 15 knots is going to be roughly equal to 17 mph.

In view of the dominant part of the mph ASI plays in your flying, you will see that the expression of speeds in this book are mainly in statute miles per hour.

Until airspeed reaches flying speed your aircraft will remain firmly on the ground. Obviously the quicker you can reach flying speed, the less will be the space required to do so. This is where wind comes in.

By pointing the aircraft **into** wind for take-off there will already be an airspeed passing over the wing to produce lift without any ground speed being generated at all.

This is best progressed diagrammatically where our aircraft reaches flying speed at 45 mph. (Fig.3)

Fig.3

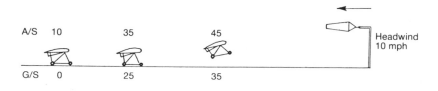

(a)   Aircraft is airborne in about three-quarters of space available.

(b)   Wind contributes to airspeed and aircraft is airborne in about half the space available.

(c)   A take-off downwind means starting off with a minus airspeed. In this situation the aircraft can run out of space before enough airspeed can be attained to sustain flight. Downwind take-offs require sufficient space to build up the faster run needed and should be thought out very carefully before being attempted.

The same situations apply to landings. Into-wind landing runs mean touching down at slower ground speeds and therefore result in shorter runs for pulling up. They allow you to land in a much smaller space.

Crosswind

A crosswind is said to exist when the wind is not directly in front of or behind the aircraft.

At take-off the aircraft's wheels are on the ground until flying speed is reached. As the crosswind meets the 'into-wind' wing the presence of dihedral will cause that wing to lift allowing a rolling movement to develop. This roll can be accelerated by the wheel acting as a pivot. (Fig.4)

Fig.4

Resultant

Roll

The result will vary according to the type of aircraft. It will either weather-cock into wind or turn and attempt to go with the wind. One way or the other there will be extreme difficulty in keeping to the original flight path. Added to this will be the likelihood of a wingtip touching the ground in the process. (Fig.4)

If flying speed has been reached the aircraft will have become airborne and unless the movement is immediately countered it will drift down wind. (Fig.5)

Wind

Drifting
Flight
Path

Fig.5

Should the windspeed momentarily drop there will be a corresponding momentary drop in airspeed and the aircraft could sink back on to the ground. In this situation the wheels will be out of line with the flight path and will strike the ground at an angle instead of head on.

The result is rather similar to that depicted in Fig.4 except the roll will be accelerated by the wheel striking the ground at an angle. (Fig.6)

Fig.6   Flight
                                  Path

Crosswind landings and take-offs are not impossible but they do require some added skill and their success will be very much governed by the cross-wind characteristics of the particular aircraft.

For example, an aircraft fitted with ailerons or spoilerons is able to lower a wing into the wind causing the wing to slip into that wind and to a large extent negate the crosswind effect.

There is no doubt that this form of control permits flying in conditions that would ground some microlights.

Wind Gradient

Meteorological and aviation text books use the term 'wind shear' when referring to changes of windspeed with height. However, for such a change near the *surface*, the term wind gradient having been used over many years in aviation will continue to be used in this book. Its effect is of crucial importance in flying a microlight or any other relatively slow aeroplane and therefore warrants the distinction from a flying if not a meteorological point of view.

The simplest way to explain wind gradient is to ask you to take a pack of playing cards and with a swinging movement drop it over a card table. The result will be self evident. The bottom card of the pack will virtually stop dead as it touches the cloth surface of the card table and each card up the pack will travel that much further than the one underneath it, with the top card travelling the most distance.

Wind behaves in the same way. Friction caused by the ground slows the wind speed at the surface with an increase taking place the higher one goes.

The true speed is reached somewhere around 2000 feet. The maximum drop in speed occurs very close to the surface and must be considered very carefully on every take-off and more so on every landing.

Another analogy based on water. A boat 'underway' at a steady speed of say 10 knots through the water suddenly meets a current of 4 knots head on. For a brief moment, due to the initial impetus of the boat, the speed through the water will be 14 knots until the effect of meeting the current has worn off and the boat reverts to a speed of 10 knots once again.

So it is with an aircraft taking off and landing. On take off it will climb into the faster moving air and show a temporary increase in airspeed. You may be tempted to reduce airspeed only to find yourself at a lower airspeed than you originally had because at that moment the effect of gradient wore off.

On landing the effect can be more critical. You are descending on the approach prior to touch down and you lower into the level of reduced wind-speed near the ground. You will feel the aircraft beginning to sink very rapidly and may be tempted to raise the nose to stop the sink; but what is happening is this. Temporarily your airspeed has dropped and should you be close to your stalling speed at the time a stall may well result particularly if you raise the nose and so increase the angle of attack. This is the last thing you want at low altitude. (Fig.7)

Fig.7

Another situation where wind gradient can have an adverse effect is when close to the ground. In a banking turn the upper wing will be travelling faster and will also be in an area of higher windspeed than the lower wing. If the speed of the lower wing falls below stalling speed whilst the upper wing continues to produce lift the result will be obvious.

Even if your airspeed is well above stalling speed the different lift forces on the respective wings can cause overbank which aileron input cannot overcome at the time. The lesson is no banking below say 150 feet.

Wind Shear

As just mentioned, in meteorological terminology wind shear is used to describe windspeed changes at different heights – in fact the name is vertical wind shear.

But the word shear can also imply change of *direction* and it is in this context we now look at it.

When conditions are right for wind shear you may be sure that they will not be right for flying a microlight.

Without delving into detail, conditions can exist in the atmosphere which give rise to sudden changes of wind direction over a minimal change of height, or even at the same height.

At great heights the effect is largely navigational but at low level it can prove critical even to the largest jet airliner set up on its final landing run.

On a conventional approach into wind you have just seen how gradient can cause a fall in airspeed. The same effect can be brought about by a change in wind direction as any such change will bring about a reduction in the value of the head wind component. (Fig.8)

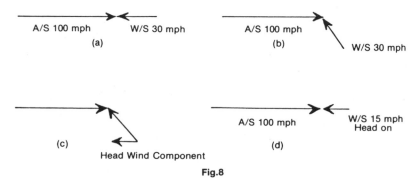

Fig.8

Taking (a) we have the normal pattern of events.

In (b) a wind shear has taken place.

At (c) you will note that the effect is now part cross and part head on as far as the aircraft is concerned.

In (d) can be seen the value of the head wind component and to all intents and purposes there has been a drop in windspeed of 15 mph.

The effect on the aircraft will be the same as that of gradient, but as shear is less predictable it is consequently more hazardous.

Normally in the landing configuration wind shear is caused by severe local thunderstorms which can have a marked effect on wind direction in a very localised area. Sufficient to say that a microlight should not be airborne in such weather.

The change in windspeed which can exist at various levels in the atmosphere is known as Vertical Wind Shear.

Low Level Turbulence

The atmosphere is rarely at rest particularly near to the ground. You have only to watch the smoke from a chimney stack to have proof of this fact.

The surface of a deep river looks placid yet it can be hiding considerable turbulence taking place on the bed. If the river is shallow the behaviour of the water close to the bed is more readily apparent. Ripples, waves and eddies caused by rocks and ruts are all visible to the eye. (Fig.9)

Fig.9

Picture the atmosphere as being this river and the 'bed' or surface the rocks and ruts are hedges, trees and buildings. Air behaving as a fluid will form the same ripples and eddies as the water and these can cause trouble for microlights. (Fig.10)

Fig.10

You should always have a mental picture of what the air can be doing when you are flying low near obstructions. Low level turbulence can be caused by another factor. Look at a fire burning out of doors. You will see air shimmering above it with particles of ash shooting upwards. This is because air, heated to a greater degree than its surroundings becomes less dense than the surrounding air and rises.

Uneven surface heating does not necessarily need fire to trigger off turbulence. An example of a natural source is simply to convey. On a sizzling hot summer day would you rather sit on a rock outcrop or on the grass? No prizes for the answer. The air around the rock is going to become much warmer than the air around the grass and consequently it will rise.

Obviously with some of the air remaining static and some on the move vertically you have a turbulent situation in the making without wind or obstructions playing a part.

On an airfield, runways, grass and buildings can all be sources of uneven heating.

You will have gathered that virtually all that has been said to date micrometeorology has been related mainly to wind. Indeed, in the early stages this is really all you need to know. To cater for the sceptics perhaps the following will highlight the problem

Type of Aircraft	Cruise Speed	Wind Speed	% Effect
Jet Airliner	600 mph	20 mph	3.33%
Light Aircraft	100 mph	20 mph	20.00%
Microlight	50 mph	20 mph	40.00%

Remember that in all the effects of wind that have been discussed the stronger the wind – the greater the effect.

Wake Turbulence

A final factor, which not specifically caused by wind but certainly associated with it in terms of avoidance, is **Wake Turbulence**.

This by definition is the disturbed air left behind any aircraft caused by propeller or jet stream and wing tip vortices. It has the power to cause total loss of control and must never be under-rated.

This area of turbulence rotates along its track widening as it does so. (Fig.11)

Fig. 11

It will track with the wind. (Fig.12)

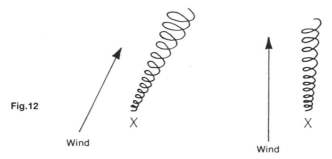

Fig.12

Wind

Wind

Normally vortices descend gradually and can exist 2 to 3 miles behind the aircraft that is the creator of the effect. They will be particularly strong with microlight aircraft. They will be affected by atmospheric conditions the nature of which from a terminology point of view is explained later in 'General Meteorology'. (Fig.13)

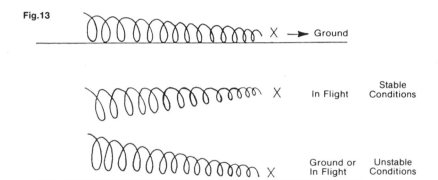

Fig.13

X ⟶ Ground

X In Flight — Stable Conditions

X Ground or In Flight — Unstable Conditions

If you are left with no alternative but to land behind another aircraft taking off then make every effort to touch down at the very beginning of the runway. This creates the largest possible gap between you and the other machine in which atmospheric conditions may have had a chance to dissipate or at least reduce the effect.

Your best method of handling wake turbulence is to avoid it at all costs by never taking off or landing immediately following another aircraft.

Bear in mind that this condition exists in flight was well as on the ground so conjure up a mental picture of its likely track. Select a path upwind of the preceding aircraft and/or below its track, according to the atmospheric conditions.

The helicopter is a particularly dangerous source of turbulence at all times.

The official figures laid down for separation in time and distance for wake turbulence are as follows.

Take-Off: From same spot as preceding aeroplane, allow 2 minutes.
From any intermediate part of the runway between the preceding aeroplane's start point on that runway and its lift off, allow 3 minutes.

No separation distances are involved at take-off.

Landing Approach: Based on the type of aeroplane you are following.

Aircraft	kg	Time	Separation
Heavy	>160,000	4 mins	8nm
Medium	>40,000	3 mins	6nm
Small	>17,000	2 mins	4nm

No official figures exist as yet for microlights but suffice to say if larger aircraft require these times and distances then the microlight pilot must certainly consider increasing them on those occasions when the risk is possible.

Remember, vortices come from induced drag and thrive on a low aspect ratio wing with a high angle of attack at low speed – all the ingredients for warning you that one microlight has to be very careful in following another.

In 'General Meteorology' which follows you will gain that further insight into the causes of weather as well as the effects – you will develop a knowledge of what makes the atmosphere behave in the way it does.

Meteorology may be an inexact science but it is a very fascinating one and it is essential that pilots are aware of the environment in which they operate.

GENERAL METEOROLOGY

The air through which you fly has weight, temperature and a moisture content. All these properties are constantly changing in value and they are the factors which combine together to produce that most talked about topic on earth – the weather.

Pressure

The weight of air from the topmost limit of the atmosphere to the surface is termed **Pressure**.

The most common unit of measurement in the UK is the Milibar (mb). However, the internaional Civil Aviation Organisation (ICAO) have changed to using the unit known as a hectoPascal (hPa) which is the same value as a millibar.

But for all practical operational purposes the UK will continue to use the unit millibar for some time to come. There is one point to note. The ICAO also lays down an **International Standard Atmosphere (ISA)** which has until now defined mean sea level pressure as 1013.25 mbs. In future, but only when reference is being made specifically to the ISA itself as an international definition, you will find the mean sea level pressure will be stated as 1013.25 hectoPascals (hPas)."

Pressure Decrease with Height

In the lower levels of the atmosphere, pressure decreases by 1 mb for approximately every 30 feet (9 metres) of ascent. After about 20 to 30,000 feet (6 to 9 kms) the ascent would need to be 50–60 feet for a pressure drop of 1 mb.

Pressure Measurement

The instrument used to measure atmospheric pressure is called a barometer, of which there are three types.

Mercury

The mercury type is the most accurate as it is devoid of mechanical parts except for a vernier scale which assists in the reading of a measurement.

It consists of a column of mercury rising from a reservoir and kept in place by the atmospheric pressure. Readings are taken from a scale alongside the column.

You may hear of pressure being talked of as being in 'inches' as a unit. This is because it was at one time measured by the number of inches of mercury in the column.

Aneroid

The aneroid type is limited in accuracy to a certain extent through the use of mechanical parts subject to friction. Basically it comprises a 'concertina' type of drum inside which air has been hermetically sealed at a fixed pressure. As the pressure inside the drum is constant the drum will contract or expand according to changes taking place in atmospheric pressure. The movements of the drum are transmitted by leverage and are shown visually on a dial (barometer) or through the trace of an inked pen on a chart placed on a rotating cylinder driven by clockwork (barograph). Both types have scales against which a reading may be taken.

Precision Aneroid

The modern observation station, previously equipped with a mercury barometer will now have a precision aneroid.

This instrument is so sensitive it will react to being moved from the floor on to a shelf – perhaps no more than five feet higher. It is sometimes referred to as a 'super-aneroid'.

Pressure Systems

Pressure readings are taken at regular intervals by day and night throughout the world at observation stations on land and at sea.

As pressure reduces with height, the altitude of each reporting station is taken into consideration so that each reading may be corrected to read as if it was at **Mean Sea Level (MSL)**.

In this way uniformity of readings is obtained from which a pressure pattern can be produced on a chart. This chart is built up by drawing lines which join places of equal MSL pressure at a given time. These lines are known as **Isobars** and they resemble contour lines on a map.

A picture of a chart could emerge thus. (Fig.1)

Weather is very much associated with pressure systems so it is necessary to have a progression of charts for forecasting purposes.

HIGH	High pressure or Anti-cyclone
LOW	Low pressure or Depression
RIDGE	Wedge or tongue of high pressure extending out from anti-cyclone
TROUGH	Similar to a ridge but extending from depression
COL	A neutral area between opposing systems.

Fig.1

Wind

Earlier under 'Wind Effect' it was said that wind was nothing more than the movement of air from areas of high pressure to areas of low pressure. High and low pressure areas lie in approximate belts around the earth. (Fig.2)

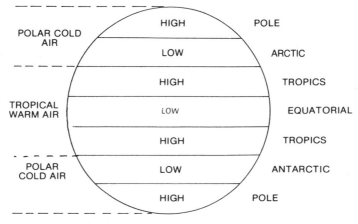

Fig.2

The rotation of the earth causes the flow to deflect and not move directly from high to low as you might expect. (Fig.3)

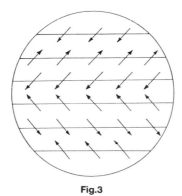

Fig.3

The rotational effect, combined with the effect of the air trying to move from high to low, results in a geostrophic effect which at 2000 ft and over causes the wind to flow around the isobars thus:

Clockwise   –   around a high (Anticyclone)
Anti-clockwise –   around a low (Depression)

This flow is known as the geostrophic wind and is depicted in Fig.4

Fig.4
FLOW AT 2000 FT.

Note – in the Southern Hemisphere these directions are reversed. Clockwise round a low and anti-clockwise round a high.

The friction of the earth's surface reduces the geostrophic effect at ground level to the extent that over land the wind blows **in** towards a Low and **out** from a High at an angle of 30° to the isobars.

Over the sea the friction is less so the angle is only 10°. (Fig.5)

Changes in wind direction are known as VEERING when clockwise and BACKING when anti-clockwise.

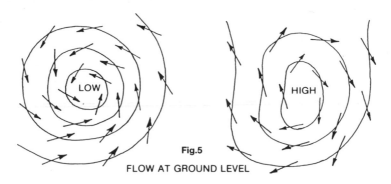

Fig.5

FLOW AT GROUND LEVEL

For example, when the wind direction changes from South-West to West it is said to have veered to the West.

∗ For those who thirst after knowledge or are gluttons for punishment we will now take a closer look into why the air moves as it does from high to low pressure and why it is deflected.

The force governing this movement is known as the 'Pressure Gradient' (not to be confused with wind gradient) and it is steep when the isobars are close together; shallow when they are relatively far apart.

Whatever the gradient, if this was the only controlling factor, the air would instantly move from high to low with an almighty rush – only dying down as the low was filled.

Observation shows otherwise. Wind does not suddenly change in speed but only over a matter of hours – sometimes days. To all intents and purposes at any given time it can be said to be constant.

Now just as with an aeroplane flying at a constant speed where thrust is balanced by drag – so there is a force which balances gradient force in a wind flow.

This balancing force is known as Coriolis effect and is a result of the earth's rotation. It is not all that easy to describe but a brave attempt will be made to do so.

Imagine an object set in motion 'downhill' from the North Pole to the Equator but not in contact with the ground. Next, imagine this object being viewed from immediately below at point A on the Equator.

As the object moves down, the observer moves to A1, due to the earth's rotation. From A1, the object will appear to have descended and moved to the left in a clockwise direction. Continue this process in viewing the object from A2, A3 and A4 and note the direction in which the object appears to be to the observer passing through each of these points. (Fig.6)

Fig.6

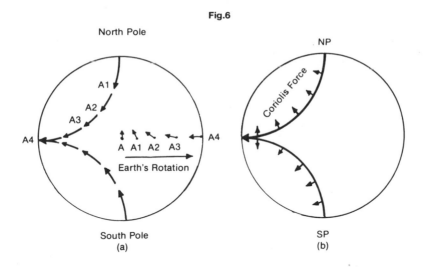

(a)

(b)

In (a) you can see the path of the object. Note how this path will be anti-clockwise if the object sets out from the South Pole.

In (b) you can see a force depicted which is acting perpendicular, or at right angles, to the object's path in order to pull it round into the curve.

This force is the Coriolis force or effect we have talked about and, you can see it is nil or neutral at the Equator.

Replace the object with a parcel of air which is on the move. As gradient and Coriolis forces must balance and as Coriolis effect is at right angles to the direction of any movement you can see why wind blows along isobars and not across same. (Fig.7)

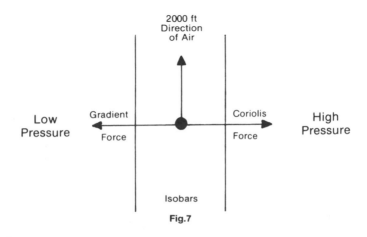

Fig.7

The above situation pre-supposes that the air is **not** in contact with the ground. Were it to be so, such contact would result in a tendency to be caught up in the rotation thus reducing the Coriolis effect as far as exactly balancing gradient force is concerned. (Fig.8)

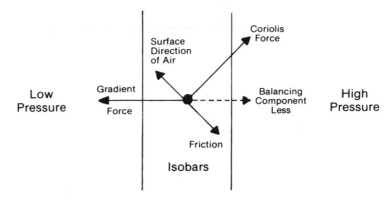

Fig.8

As Coriolis effect is always at right angles to any movement path you can see how the shift in Coriolis causes a change in wind direction at the earth's surface. Friction now plays a part in the balancing force needed to maintain a constant wind speed as you have just seen.

**

On an Ordnance Survey map where the contours are close together they are depicting a steep rise or fall of ground. So it is with isobars on the chart – the closer they are together the steeper the rise or fall in pressure over a given distance and in consequence the stronger are the winds.

A rough guide to a centre of low pressure's position is to stand with your back to the wind – the centre will be to your left.

The rule is very useful in another way. You are flying with a strong wind on your port side. This is indicative of flying towards a low pressure centre which in turn means that your altimeter will begin to read high. If you are not aware of what is happening you could adjust your altitude to maintain a constant reading and in conditions of poor visibility in the vicinity of high ground this would be very dangerous as you would be descending.

Apart from winds caused by pressure systems over a large area there are also more localised winds often appearing contrary in direction to the prevailing wind at the time.

Sea Breeze Effect – The air over the land heats more quickly than the air over the sea. The warm air rises and the cooler air from the sea flows in to replace it. The effect does not normally penetrate far inland but there are exceptions.

Convection Wind   – Similar to sea breeze effect but can occur anywhere. Uneven heating causes air to rise and cooler air flows in from all round to fill the gap. The sudden lifting of a windsock on a calm summer day is often an indication of a convection wind. It is shortly followed by a return to calm as a balance is restored. More on this later.

Katabatic Wind   – Colder air from the tops of mountains, being more dense rolls down the slopes into the lower ground of valleys. This phenomenon is more frequent at night.

Anabatic Wind   – Air in valleys warms up more quickly than air on the mountain tops. This less dense air then moves up the valleys and slopes rather as air moves upward due to uneven heating. An anabatic wind is sometimes referred to as a Valley Breeze.

Hill Lift

Wind has so far been talked about as being more of an enemy than a friend. However, you are now considered to be much more experienced and ready to make use of the opportunities that wind can sometimes offer.

Ask any glider or hang glider pilot what they think about hill lift and they will normally go into raptures as it is a prime way in which they can remain airborne for virtually as long as they like.

Many microlights are akin to gliders and hang gliders in that in spite of the added weight of an engine they still have a very reasonable gliding angle when the power is off.

Hill lift is a component acting as a result of wind being forced up a slope. (Fig.9)

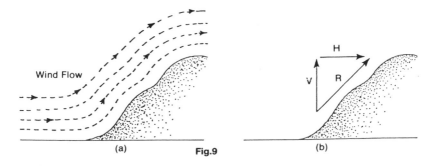

Wind Flow

(a)   **Fig.9**   (b)

In (a) you are looking at the obvious – wind moving up and over a hill lying in its path.

In (b) you are looking at a breakdown of the forces involved.

R – the resultant caused by the hill.

H – a horizontal component of that resultant.

V – a vertical component of that resultant and the most important one as far as we are concerned.

For example, a wind travelling at around 30 ft per second (20 mph) up a 45° slope could produce a vertical component of some 20 f.p.s. in a given area above the slope.

Gliding down at 20 f.p.s. through the air which is rising at say 30 f.p.s. would result in your aircraft ascending in relation to the ground at a rate of 10 f.p.s. as long as it remained in that rising air.

The area of best hill lift is usually to be found about one-third out from the top of the hill in relation to the foot of the hill.

It does not take much imagination to realise the opportunities that hill lift offers the microlight pilot. With the engine throttled right back a considerable amount of air time can be enjoyed with the minimum amount of fuel being used.

There have been occasions when light aircraft pilots with soaring experience have made use of hill lift in times of engine trouble. They have been able to stretch their flights giving more time to select a suitable forced landing site and in some cases they have actually been able to reach their destination where it has been in the vicinity of the hill range.

What goes up must come down – there is always the other side of the hill. Just as air will climb as it meets the windward slope so it will descend down the leeward side. This time the vertical component will be acting in the opposite direction – it will not be lift, it will be a downdraft.

You must be ever conscious of your position in relation to hills. On the leeward side you may be cruising at the correct airspeed only to find yourself descending at an unhealthy rate in relation to the ground.

An instinctive reaction at that moment may be to climb which could lead to a stall – the downdraft may be too powerful for your aircraft's engine to pull you up. There is only one course of action you must take – act contrary to instinct, increase your airspeed and head downwind away from the slope to escape the effect. (Fig.10)

Fig.10

Rotor Effect

A far worse situation can be encountered should the lee side be in the form of a relatively sudden drop. Remember the river bed where in the immediate vicinity of rocks and ruts there were eddies set up – not smooth ripples.

The smooth flow will break up and the air will behave quite wildly creating a rotor effect in which you may not only be forced down but also lose control in the rough air. (Fig.11)

Fig.11

Wave Effect

Turn your thoughts to the river once again. When ripples are created by an obstruction they can carry on downstream reaching quite long distances from the cause.

So it is with the air. Given certain atmospheric conditions the air will travel in a wave motion for some considerable way downwind from the hills that set the motion in being. (Fig.12)

Fig.12

Standing waves as they are called can reach to considerable heights and are much used by sailplane pilots wanting to cover long distances. Each wave will produce lift on its windward side and a downdraft on the leeward side.

The uninitiated power pilot is often bewildered to find his rate of ascent or descent quite dramatically changing although the cruising speed and engine revs are constant and there are no hills in the immediate vicinity. If a quick look at the map indicates hills some distance upwind then a wave should be presumed and the flight path adjusted up or downwind to a point out of the wave effect.

If this effect is experienced in closer proximity to the hills then the move should be downwind only – to avoid any rotor problems that could arise in the immediate lee of those hills.

Temperature

Contrary to popular belief the atmosphere is not heated directly by the sun. The sun heats the earth and the earth heats the atmosphere on the principle of a radiator.

This fact is made more apparent when one realises that the higher one goes the colder it becomes – in other words, one is colder on moving away from the 'radiator'.

The seasons play a part in the amount of heat put into the radiator. In summer, in the British Isles, the sun is high in the sky and the days are long. In winter, the sun is at a low angle and the days are short. Naturally, the longer the sunshine each day, the hotter becomes the 'radiator'. (Fig.13)

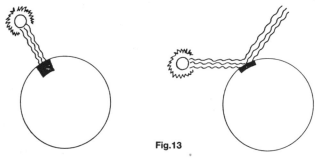

Fig.13

Cloud acts as an insulator – it can reduce the amount of heat taken in and it can also reduce the amount that radiates or escapes into the atmosphere at night.

Temperature is now reported in **Celsius** (also known as Centigrade) and is expressed in degrees (°C); the Fahrenheit scale is virtually extinct.

The ISA temperature is defined as 15°C at mean sea level (MSL).

Lapse Rate

Lapse Rate (LR) is the name given to the rate at which temperature drops with height. It is constantly changing according to the nature of the air mass existing at the time.

It is important in forecasting so regular readings above given locations are taken several times a day by aircraft or balloons equipped with radio.

Inversion

A situation where temperature is seen to increase with height. This is usually the result of warm air, which is less dense, climbing over colder air. It can also come about nearer the ground when the ground cools rapidly in the evening through radiation and the air immediately in contact with the ground is colder than that above. Inversions are particularly noted for trapping fog and haze and causing bad visibility. They are normally associated with anti-cyclones.

Adiabatic Lapse Rate

When an amount or 'parcel' of air is *forced* to ascend or descend it will be affected by a decrease or increase in pressure. Before we go any further, consider the following analogies.

When using a bicycle pump you will soon be aware of how hot it becomes with not any extra heat being introduced around it. Without having to delve into the realms of physics, you can experience the fact that as pressure is increased inside the pump – so is the temperature.

The reverse happens when a decrease in pressure takes place – there is a loss of temperature even if there is no external loss of heat introduced to the surround. The way a refrigerator can work demonstrates this where the removal of air reduces pressure and thus creates the required chill.

Having established these facts we can proceed.

So when a 'parcel' of air within the atmosphere is forced to ascend through having to cross over hills or by uneven heating as discussed earlier the pressure will decrease and the temperature will do likewise. This form of cooling, with no outside factor involved except the decrease in pressure, is known as **Adiabatic Cooling**. This cooling takes place at *fixed* rates for dry and wet air.

The difference between dry and wet air for our purposes is as follows:

Dry air is air which may contain moisture but has not yet reached the point where the moisture content condenses into cloud.

Wet air is air whose moisture content has condensed into cloud.

Having established the distinction it is possible to give figures for the two adiabatic lapse rates.

Dry Adiabatic Lapse Rate (DALR) is a constant 3° per 1000 feet.

Saturated (Wet) Adiabatic Lapse Rate (SALR) is a constant 1.5° per 1000 feet until at about 6000 feet where it begins to increase. Finally at around 30,000 feet it will be the same as the DALR.

Why the difference you may ask? The best analogy to describe this occurrence is to ask you to recall what happens when you have washed your hair and you then apply an electric dryer to it. Alternatively, recall how you feel on coming out of the sea on a hot summer day as you lie on the beach to dry.

In both cases you will feel a distinct coolness until you are dry. The reason is that evaporation, which is what is happening, uses up heat – hence the cooling effect. To explain the difference in the two adiabatic lapse rates we must look at the opposite to evaporation, namely condensation.

When condensation takes place heat is given off known as latent heat. This latent heat is sufficient to reduce the rate of cooling in air where condensation is taking place by about half. Hence to 1.5° in saturated conditions compared with 3° dry – until around 6000 ft.

The different types of lapse rates are important in understanding the formation of cloud so no excuses are offered for elaborating on the subject.

Incidentally, before moving on, do bear in mind that similar changes take place within descending air where the process would now be termed **Adiabatic Warming**.

Relative Humidity

This was touched on slightly in discussing lapse rates. Relative humidity is the amount of water vapour present in a given mass of air expressed as a percentage of the total amount of water vapour that mass could hold before becoming saturated.

Temperature has a great bearing on the amount of water vapour the air can hold. (Fig.14)

Fig.14

Take a mass of air at a given temperature and assume that this air contains 50% of the total water vapour it can hold. It is thus said to have a relative humidity of 50%. (Fig.14a)

When cooled, air can contain less water vapour. Hence, the same water vapour content *increases* relative to the maximum amount of such vapour in the air can hold. (Fig.14b)

On yet further cooling the water vapour content can eventually reach the point where the air is only just able to contain it. The air is now said to be saturated with a relative humidity of 100%. (Fig.14c)

The temperature at which the air becomes saturated is known as the **dew point** temperature.

Still further cooling will produce more water vapour than the air can hold. At this point **condensation** can take place where the excess invisible water vapour converts into visible water particles as cloud. If at ground level, it will be fog or dew. (Fig.14d)

For any condensation to take place there must be minute particles of matter (e.g. dust) present in the atmosphere – known as **condensation nuclei**.

Air Masses

An air mass is no more than its name implies – a mass of air. It is its characteristics that are important and these are acquired from the region of the earth's surface over which it forms.

Such regions are known as **source regions** and they are usually associated with the centre of a slow moving anti-cyclone; where the stable conditions allow the air to stagnate and absorb the characteristics of the source region.

As the main anti-cyclone belts are to be found in the polar and tropical latitudes of the world, it will not come as a surprise to know that there are two basic types of air mass – polar and tropical. But the distinction does not stop there.

Where stagnation takes place over land, the air will be relatively dry whilst over sea areas it will become moist due to evaporation.

This produces two further sub-types of air mass – dry, known as continental and moist, known as maritime. (Fig.15)

Polar Maritime
(Cold Moist)

Polar Continental
(Cold Dry)

Tropical Continental
(Warm Dry)

Tropical Maritime
(Warm Moist)

Fig.15

We thus end up with four main types:

Polar Maritime	–	Cold/Moist
Polar Continental	–	Cold/Dry
Tropical Maritime	–	Warm/Moist
Tropical Continental	–	Warm/Dry

As you can see the British Isles lies in a 'Pig in the Middle' situation in that they all too frequently experience the influence of all four types of air mass. Because of this they lend themselves to being a good subject for the study of weather. No doubt their geographical position has led to the old adage – 'the climate in Britain is really quite pleasant – it's the weather that's so b..... awful!'

When one pressure system (a high or a low) gains dominance over another air from the air mass begins to travel. This is known as an **Airstream**. Note, at times the word Airmass is used to mean Airstream as well.

On route it will take on any different characteristics it finds by changes in the surface over which it passes.

This process is known as **Transformation**.

Naturally the extent of transformation depends not only on the differing surfaces over which it travels but also the length of time it takes to do so.

An excellent example of transformation sometimes takes place in proximity to the British Isles when a large depression – or low – is centred to the west and a polar maritime airstream is heading south (Fig.16)

Fig.16

Polar

Low

Tropical

Tropical maritime air
in lower layers.

The air mass can be moved sufficiently far south to take up tropical characteristics from the warmer seas – at least tropic in characteristics in the lower layers.

When this situation arises the airstream is known as a **Returning Polar Maritime** airstream. (Airmass)

Any polar maritime airstream will always undergo a measure of transformation on moving south over a relatively warmer sea though not maybe to the extent exampled above.

However, the journey over sea may be shorter with little or no opportunity to warm up. This occurs when a polar maritime airstream comes down on to the British Isles directly from the north. The result is a really cold blast indeed and such a flow is known as an **Arctic Maritime** airstream. (airmass)

The various airstreams in relation to the pressure centres responsible for their movement are shown in Fig.17.

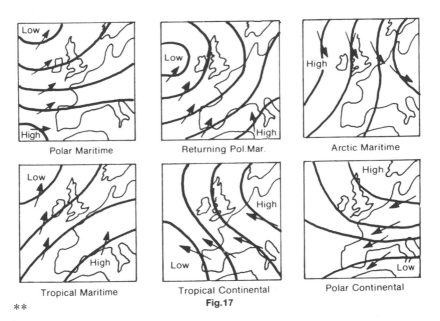

Polar Maritime   Returning Pol.Mar.   Arctic Maritime

Tropical Maritime   Tropical Continental   Polar Continental

Fig.17

**

Fronts

The British Isles once again present themselves as a good example for our next discussion, lying as they do at the approximate meeting point of the Arctic Low and Tropical High pressure belts depicted in Fig.2 on Page 142.

As one or the other of these belts gains dominance at a given time so the systems caused (Highs, Lows, etc.) move the differing air masses into contact with each other. The meeting point in this 'battle zone' is known as a front, where a 'kink' can occur as warm air makes an incursion into the cold air. (Fig.18)

Fig.18

Fronts are normally associated with depressions which usually move from west to east. They appear on a weather map thus. (Fig.19)

Fig.19

The warm front moves faster than the cold air before it and being warmer (less dense) it climbs up over it. The following cold front slowly overtakes the warm air but being colder (more dense) it undercuts it and forces it up. A cross section at ground level would look thus. (Fig.20)

Fig.20

When the cold air finally overtakes the warm air the front is said to have been 'occluded'. (Fig.21)

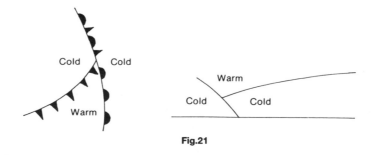

Fig.21

It was said earlier that fronts are normally associated with depressions. A picture of how the relationship would appear on a chart is shown in Fig.22.

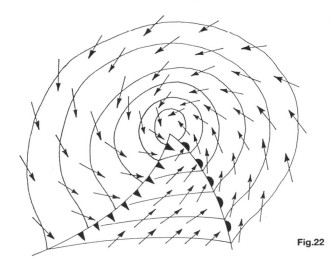

Fig.22

Particularly notice how the fronts cause a 'kink' in the isobars – there can be a distinct veer in the wind as a front passes.

The Troposphere

Cloud formation and weather only occur within a limited belt of the atmosphere.

This belt is known as the **Troposphere** and is noted from the rest of the atmosphere by the fact that within it there is a definite temperature lapse rate which by the ISA standard is accepted as 2°C per 1000 ft (1.98° to be exact) up to the **Tropopause**.

The tropopause is the transition line, not a belt, between the Troposphere and the Stratosphere.

Above the tropopause lies the **Stratosphere** where, in its lower layers up to around 69,000 ft (21 km), the temperature can be relatively constant.

Referring back to the tropopause, its height above the Earth's surface, and therefore the depth of the troposphere, in the temperate latitudes is around 36,000 ft (11 kms). This figure varies considerably with the regions being only about 30,000 ft (9 km) at the Poles but over 52,000 ft at the Equator.

Similarly, the tropopause is affected by the seasons – being higher in summer and lower in winter.

It is also higher above the warm sector of a frontal system.

These variations are shown in Fig.23.

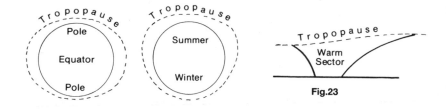

Fig.23

From a flying point of view the variations in the tropopause may seem academic. However, you have only to experience a tropical thunderstorm to realise how convection being able to reach higher levels can produce much more violent weather. To a lesser extent you can witness a quite effective example in the British Isles by noting the height to which Cu Nimb reach up in summer compared with winter.

Clouds

When talking about clouds we are entering into the more visible aspects of meteorology. Wind or temperature we can feel and experience its effect but cloud we can actually see and, with experience, be able to interpret the signs each types provides.

Clouds are classified by the height of their base. The three classifications and their base heights are officially defined as follows:

Low cloud	Surface	to 6,500 ft (2 km)
Medium cloud	6,500 ft (2 km)	to 23,000 ft (7 km)
High cloud	16,000 ft (5 km)	to 45,000 ft (14 km)

The wide range of base heights stems from the variations in the height of the tropopause according to location in the world and/or the season.

In the UK, reasonable approximations in feet could be around:

	Low	Medium	High
Summer	5,000	16,000	25,000
Winter	1,000	6,500	16,000

Within these broad classifications there are particular types.

Types of cloud

Low Cloud

Stratus St
— A layer or sheet of cloud of varying thickness which is sometimes associated with drizzle or light rain.
— Stratus in the early morning during summer will usually herald a good day as soon as the sun can burn it away.

- In winter it can persist all day and produce the condition known as 'Anti-cyclonic Gloom'.
- Fog is Stratus whose base is at ground level.

Nimbo-Stratus
N St
- A dense sheet of amorphous shaped layer cloud whose thickness can extend up into medium cloud levels.
- It is associated with continuous rain preceding a warm front.

Fracto-Nimbus
F Nim
- The air below Nimbo-Stratus can become saturated by the rain passing through it and it condenses into ragged fragments of cloud often referred to as 'scud cloud'.

Strato Cumulus
St Cu
- Patches of cloud, 'lumpy' in appearance but with no great thickness or particular shape.
- It is not indicative of any particular weather.
- It can produce light rain if thick enough when associated with certain types of front.

Small Cumulus
Cu
- Small puffy cloud whose base is always flat and the top is rounded.
- The length of the base is greater than the height.
- Also known as 'Fair weather cloud'.

Large Cumulus
Cu
- A cumulus cloud whose height exceeds the width of the base. Easily recognisable as towering cloud with 'cauliflower' shaped tops.
- As long as the tops are crisp in outline it is still active. Once they become ragged then growth has stopped.
- Large Cumulus produce showers which can be heavy or light according to the size of the cloud.
- The tops can extend up into medium cloud levels above.

Cumulo Nimbus
Cb
- These are large cumulus which have climbed into the high cloud levels where the tops become ice crystals known as 'false cirrus'.
- The top of a Cu-Nimb is very distinctive as it spreads out in an anvil shape on hitting the invisible roof of equilibrium (of which more will be said later). The anvil moves downwind faster than the rest of the cloud as the winds at the upper level are usually stronger.

– Violent weather is normally associated with this cloud and certainly no microlight should be in the air when it is around.

– Thunderstorms, hail, heavy rain and squalls are all products of these clouds.

– Surface winds can alter to a considerable extent in terms and direction in their vicinity producing wind shear effect.

– May be associated with cold fronts where the warm air being undercut is unstable. They can often be hidden by other cloud formed in the warm sector set up by the warm front that passed previously.

– They are more likely to be found in an unstable polar maritime airstream or at the breakdown of a heat wave.

Mammatus
Mamma

– Forms under the anvil of a Cu Nimb or Alto-Cumulus.
They appear as 'inverted cumulus' with an udder-like shape.

Medium Cloud

Alto-Cumulus
Ac

– Is Strato-Cumulus at medium height level (Above 6500 feet).

– At times it can form into a pattern known as a 'Mackerel sky'.

Alto Cumulus
Cumulus Genitus
AcCu-CuGen

– Alto Cumulus formed by large cumulus spreading out on reaching equilibrium (more later).

– Can cover a large area of the sky thus cutting of the sun's rays and so reducing thermal activity.

– On occasions it can develop into mammatus.

Alto-Stratus
A St

– Stratus at medium height level.

– Should it appear to be lowering and thickening from the west there is very probably a warm front on the way bringing Nimbo-Stratus and rain.

Alto-Cumulus
Lenticularis
Ac Lent

– Cigar-shaped, medium cloud formed by standing waves in the lee of mountain ranges.

– Lenticular clouds do not move with the wind across the sky like other clouds. They appear at the crest of each wave.

Alto-Cumulus Castellanus Ac Cast	– This is a form of Alto-Cumulus which usually appears after a very hot spell. It is distinctive by its hard turreted outline. – It is a warning that unstable thundery conditions are developing and could break out in a day or so. – Can appear and disappear several times prior to the thundery outbreaks occurring.

High Cloud

Cirrus Ci	– Due to the freezing temperatures at their height, Cirrus type clouds are composed of ice crystals. – A fibrous looking cloud, the most well known form being known as 'Mares Tails' – streaks which turn up at one end.
Cirro-Stratus Ci St	– Stratus at high level. – If seen thickening and lowering into Alto-Stratus in the west it is the first sign of a warm front on its way.
Cirro-Cumulus Ci Cu	– Similar to Alto-Cumulus in looks but usually composed of ice crystals or ice particles. – Also forms the 'Mackerel sky' pattern. – Usually associated with quiet weather.

A sketch of cloud types can be found in Fig.24.

The Forming of Cloud

Referring back to relative humidity you will recall that when a mass of air was cooled to its dew point temperature, the water vapour content became 100% and any further cooling resulted in condensation into visible water particles given that condensation nuclei was present of course.

To establish how cloud is formed is simply a matter of examining the various ways in which a mass of air can be cooled to its dew point.

We will look at three different ways in which this can be brought about.

Convection

Easily the most fascinating way in which cloud can be formed, certainly the most important from the point of view of the sailplane and hang glider pilot fraternity from whom we are not too far removed.

Convection is triggered off by causing a mass of air to become warmer than its surround. One method by which this can come about was touched

CLOUD TYPES

Fig.24

upon in 'Wind Effect', namely that of uneven heating. Recall the analogy of the rock outcrop and the grass on a hot summer day.

Different substances have varying capacities for heat and the measurement of such capacity is in terms of specific heat. This is the amount of heat required to raise the temperature of a given unit of substance by one degree.

As an example of varying specific heats, take water and copper. An equal amount of heat applied to a unit of water to raise its temperature by 1° would raise the temperature of an equivalent unit of copper by 11°.

Hence you can see how the same amount of sunshine falling on different surfaces will raise their temperature according to the specific heat value of the substance of which each surface is composed.

However, our concern is with the effect of uneven heating rather than its cause.

Air in immediate contact with a surface warmer than surrounding surfaces will itself become warmer than the surrounding air. On warming it will become less dense that its environment, will break away and rise. (Fig.25)

Fig.25

We must now take into account the difference lapse rates discussed earlier as they are the key to what takes place in this situation.

First there is the lapse rate of the atmosphere which is in a state of change from time to time and place to place – hence the regular readings that have to be taken as described earlier to update the **Environmental Lapse Rate (ELR)** as it is called.

Then we have the Dry Adiabatic Lapse Rate which is a constant 3° per 1000 ft (DALR). Air forced to rise within its surround will cool at this rate.

An example of what could take place is thus. (Fig.26)
In the foregoing example where the ELR is greater than the DALR conditions are said to be unstable.

Had the ELR been less than the DALR the warmer air on trying to rise would have quickly become cooler than its surround and would have fallen back to the surface before gaining any height; conditions would have been said to have been Stable. (Fig.27)
We must now consider what happens when the rising air reaches Dew Point level – the level where the temperature is such that the water vapour can condense into water particles.

HEIGHT IN FEET	ELR PER 1000	AIR TEMP PER 1000	DALR PER 1000	TEMP. OF RISING AIR
6000'		−2.0°		−2.5°
	2°		3°	
5000'		0°		0.5°
	2°		3°	
4000'		2°		3.5°
	3°		3°	
3000'		5°		6.5°
	3°		3°	
2000'		8°		9.5°
	3°		3°	
1000'		11°		12.5°
	4°		3°	
GROUND		15°		15.5°

EQUILIBRIUM SAME TEMP. AS SURROUND

AIR BREAKS AWAY AND RISES

UNEVEN HEATING

Fig.26

TEMPERATURES IN CENTIGRADE

	ATMOSPHERE-ELR	RISING AIR	ADIABATIC LAPSE RATE
2000'	13°		
1000'	14°	12.5°	
GROUND	15°	15.5°	DALR 3°

Fig.27

Remember, as condensation takes place latent heat is given off which effectively reduces the cooling rate of the rising air by half – certainly up to 6000 ft. The cooling rate in the cloud now becomes that of the Saturated Adiabatic Lapse Rate at 1.5° per 1000 ft. (SALR).

The cloud produced by convection is of the Cumulus type and, with the reduction in cooling due to latent heat, the height which Cumulus clouds reach can be very great indeed before equilibrium comes about. (Fig.28)

TEMPERATURES IN CENTIGRADE

Fig.28

Thermal Lift

It is appropriate to digress here for a moment from what convection is to what convection can do for pilots. At the beginning it was said that convection was certainly important to glider and hang glider enthusiasts. The reason is simple – convection brings about rising air and use can be made of this as it is in hill lift.

Unlike hill lift the rising air in convection is not a broad expanse related to a geographical feature; it is in fact a 'column' in shape and is known as a **Thermal**. Many microlight aircraft are quite capable of making use of thermals.

If a thermal ascends at say 20 ft per second and your glide rate of 10 fps then by remaining in the core of the thermal you will gain height relative to the ground at the rate of 10 fps. (Fig.29)
Eventually you will glide out of the bottom of the thermal and will have to start the process again with another thermal. Because the thermal is a column, keeping in the core requires correct circling which can only come with experience unless you have access to a two-seater and an instructor to pass on the 'know-how'.

There are some 'wrinkles' for recognising thermals. In level flight or a steady glide you suddenly feel a surge of airspeed and a feeling like being on a boat which is lifted bodily by a wave.

165

THERMAL + 20FPS
GLIDE − 10FPS
_____
GAIN + 10FPS

AS LONG AS THE AIRCRAFT
REMAINS IN THE THERMAL

AIRCRAFT DESCENDING
THROUGH THERMAL

Fig.29

If you have a variometer or a vertical speed indicator you will notice that they register ascent at that moment.

At this moment you have to circle to left or right in an endeavour to keep within the thermal's core where the lift is greatest. If on first sensing the lift you experienced a wing being lifted up then it is fair to assume that the core lies towards the wing that was affected and you would turn accordingly in that direction.

Before you can recognise a thermal you have to be astute enough to detect likely sources.

In summer the most likely places would be rock outcrops, villages, or dry sandy surfaces followed by vegetation covered land with little or no activity over water.

In winter the most vigorous thermal activity takes place over the sea.

An obvious solution is to fly under any developing Cumulus clouds but if there are no clouds then watch other aircraft or birds. If they look to be on the up and up, go in and join their circle. Having said this, the comparatively poor visibility from some microlights in an upward direction demands that you do this with extreme care.

Another solution is to question pilots as to where they feel the good thermal sources are to be found in that locality. However, you must remember that when a thermal breaks away it travels horizontally with the wind as well as upwards. In all but dead calm conditions its path will always be a slope. (Fig.30)

So much for the digression. Reverting back to the ways in which cloud can be formed we come to the next set of conditions.

Fig.30

Orographic Cloud

Air on meeting mountains rises to pass over them. As it does so it will cool adiabatically and condense if dew point level is reached.

Two types of cloud will basically be the outcome of any condensation that takes place depending on the ELR at the same time. Both will be said to be **orographic**.

– Stratiform cloud in the form of Stratus or Strato-Cumulus if conditioned are stable. Such cloud forming below the hill top is designated hill fog.
– Cumiliform cloud if the conditions are unstable and convection is triggered off by the rising air.

Examples are shown in Fig.31.

Fig.31

You will recall that mountain ranges can set up standing waves. Just as such ranges can produce cloud in their proximity so the waves that are created can do likewise.

Where dew point level is just below the crest of the wave, the air travelling up to the crest cools and condenses producing cloud. This cloud will immediately evaporate as the air warms up on travelling down the other side of the crest.

The clouds so produced are of a most distinctive shape known as Lenticular clouds. They lie across the wind and can exist for great distances downwind of the mountain range that caused them. (Fig.32)

They are usually at medium cloud level, are cigar-like in shape and easily recognisable because they do not move with the wind; they remain stationary at the crest.

Fig.32

Being at medium height they are probably only of academic interest to the microlight pilot. On the other hand, wave effect can be experienced in the lower levels so they could be taken as indicative of wave effect being about.

To the sailplane pilot they are a veritable signpost to standing waves and subsequent distance goals.

Now to the remaining cause of cloud.

Clouds Associated with Fronts

Fronts are capable of producing most of the cloud types listed.

At a front it is the warm air which is predominantly responsible for the formation of cloud as it can contain so much more water vapour than the colder air.

Cloud is formed by:
– Warm air cooling on climbing over relatively colder air (Warm Front)
– Warm air cooling on rising at being undercut by relatively colder air (cold front).

A 'text book' picture of a classical warm and cold front cloud situation is shown in Fig.33.

Would that life was like Fig.33; prediction would be so simple. Unfortunately text-book situations are like average situations – they rarely occur.

The atmosphere is usually in constant motion – wind is a perfect example of this in the horizontal sense. There is also a vertical motion but the speed is not even remotely the same as wind.

This particular vertical motion is distinctly separate from convection.

You will recall that cloud is formed by rising air, cooling as it does so, and condensing at dew point level. Conversely, when air descends, it warms, can contain more moisture and therefore disperses cloud or precludes it from forming.

It is this albeit very slow vertical motion up or down which causes the formation or dispersal of most types of layer cloud at all levels.

So how does this affect our 'text book' fronts?

Cold Front Gradient 1:50   Warm Front Gradient 1:150

In the cold sector as cold wet air comes down from the North West the bottom of the mass is warmed and convection sets in to produce cumulus of all types with showers.

The cold front being denser sharply undercuts the warm air causing a short spell of heavy rain, squalls or even thunder. A further veer of wind.

The situation depicted is known as a 'classical' cold front and pre-supposes the warm air is unstable.

As the Warm Front goes through the rain slackens off and shapeless Nimbo Stratus becomes Stratus and Strato-Cumulus. The wind veers with the passing of the Front. Drizzle may occur.

Continuous rain from lowering Nimbo Stratus - can go on for some hours depending on speed of Front.

Cirro Stratus has lowered to form Alto Stratus and rain may be visible far to the West. Little or no low cloud will be present.

Cirrus in the West thickens into Cirro-Stratus as warm air climbs up over the colder air. Any convection cloud begins to die out.

(COLD) →

LARGE CUMULUS

FR. NIMBUS

CUMULO NIMBUS

ST.CU. STRATUS

(WARM) →

FR. STRATUS

NIMBO STRATUS

ALTO STRATUS

CIRRO STRATUS

(COLD) →

CUMULUS CUMULUS CUMULUS

Pressure continues to rise.

Pressure starts to rise.

Pressure drop eases or levels off.

Pressure drop continues.

Rate of drop shows the intensity of the depression.

Pressure begins to drop.

Any Cumulus begins to decline as convection is damped.

Fig.33

Should there be a descending movement in the warm air at a front, the depth to which the cloud extends will be stunted.

Compared with the warm front depicted in Fig.33 the picture will be more like this. (Fig.34)

Fig.34
Kata Warm Front

The above type of front is called a **Kata Warm Front**.

Earlier when we discussed wind we talked about Katabatic and Anabatic winds. The former descended down the hill whilst the latter blew up it. Hence, in describing a front we call it a Kata warm front if warm air is descending and an Ana warm front if it is ascending.

The 'text book' warm front in Fig.33 is an **Ana Warm Front**. The cloud depth is very great due to the warm moist air ascending without restraint to high cloud (Cirrus) levels.

Cold fronts are also affected by whether the warm air is descending or ascending as it is undercut by colder air. You can therefore have Kata or Ana cold fronts.

In a **Kata Cold Front**, once again the depth of cloud is minimised by the descending warm air. (Fig.35)

Fig.35
Kata Cold Front

Finally we are left with the **Ana Cold Front** to complete the picture – that is, colder air under-cutting ascending warm air.

This form of front manifests itself in two distinct ways according to whether the warm air is unstable or not.

If the air is unstable then you will see the classical cold front produced. This is shown in Fig.33.

However, in Britain such a situation seldom arises as warm air masses are rarely unstable. Also, the warm air is usually descending.

If the warm air is stable the picture is simply the reverse of the Ana warm front in Fig.33. Except the width of the front is around only one-third to one-half of the warm front belt. (Fig.36)

Fig.36
Ana Cold Front

The Ana cold front in Fig.36 does occur in Britain but mostly during the winter months.

There is one distinctive feature common to both types of Ana cold front. The rear edge of the associated cloud mass is very clear-cut, particularly at high levels. In fact it can appear as a virtual straight line right across the sky.

The demarcation of weather types is also more clearly defined – as is the transition from warm to cold air and the veer in wind direction.

Kata fronts are less vigorous in terms of weather and rainfall amounts – be they warm or cold. Also, all the changes just elaborated upon are much slower in taking place and are more ill-defined.

To sum up, no two fronts are ever likely to be exactly the same – neither will be the clouds associated with them.

However, from a flying point of view they must be treated with caution. Unless a front is very weak, rainfall, low cloud and poor visibility are a racing certainty. Poor visibility is particularly hazardous as not only can it hide hills but, as a warm front passes, it could mean you are less likely to spot that very dangerous unstable cold front that could be lurking in the offing.

Always be prepared to abandon your plans to fly. It is better to be on the ground wishing you were in the air than to be in the air wishing to heaven you were on the ground!

Icing

We will start with a few points on ice itself. Just as condensation nuclei is a prerequisite for condensation to take place, so there is a need for **freezing nuclei** to be present for ice to form.

The process of transforming water vapour into ice crystals is known chemically as deposition but in meteorological circles it is referred to as **sublimation**.

Without the presence of freezing nuclei, water droplets can remain in liquid form well under 0°C. They are then known as **super-cooled** droplets or particles (depending on size) but they will usually turn to ice on striking an object.

Such droplets, lifted up to cirrus level in a cu-nimb cloud can transform into ice crystals by the process known as **glaciation**.

And so on to the forms of icing that can relate to aviation.

Hoar Frost – Ice crystals formed by sublimation on to a cold surface with a temperature below 0°C. It can occur on an aircraft when parked or when descending from below freezing level into warmer moister air. Such frost or any similar deposit must be removed totally from an aircraft prior to flight. Not only does it add extra weight but it can jeopardise lift by distorting the smooth flow of air over the wing.

Rime Ice – Flight through cloud with a relatively low moisture content containing super-cooled water particles can produce rime ice as the particles freeze on striking the aircraft. The icing will be in the form of a white opaque deposit confined to the leading edge of the wing and its immediate surround. (Fig.37) As it builds up the airflow can begin to break it away but sufficient can remain to disturb the smooth airflow over the wing affecting lift and thereby the stall speed.

Rime ice is usually associated with stratiform cloud where the super-cooled particles are small.

Fig.37

Clear Ice – Also called **glazed ice**, this is the most hazardous form of all. When an aircraft is flying through dense towering cu and cunimb cloud it will be striking very large super-cooled droplets indeed.

Initially, on striking the aircraft, only *part* of the droplet will freeze instantly for the following reason. Recall how latent heat is given off when condensation takes place; so, further latent heat is released when a liquid changes into a solid.

This heat delays total freezing of the droplet momentarily, thus enabling the still liquid part of the droplet to flow back over a wing (or other flying surface).

Although it will virtually freeze as it flows it will now be covering a much larger area and with repetition of the process, as more droplets strike the aircraft, the aerofoil shape of the wing can be severely distorted to a much greater extent than it would be by rime ice – not to mention the additional weight. This **ice accretion** as it is called will have a major detrimental, in fact dangerous, effect on the aircraft's handling and stall speed.

Rain Ice – Similar to clear or glazed ice but on this occasion the aircraft will be flying in sub-zero temperature *outside* cloud but through rain falling from relatively warmer moist air above. Should the raindrops become super-cooled in falling through the freezing temperature they will freeze on striking the already sub-zero surface of the aircraft. (Fig.38)

Warm Air

Sub-Zero Air

Nimbo Stratus

Fig.38

Weather

Normally you would not be flying in 'weather' as it is referred to here. Nevertheless there is always the need for understanding as much about the sky as possible when you are 'hooked' on taking the odd excursion into it.

Rain – When condensation continues to produce more and more water particles they join up to become larger in size until finally they are too heavy for the rising currents in the cloud to support them. They fall in the form of rain.

– Should the ability to hold them up be too weak before they become as large as rain drops, they will fall before reaching any size at all – this is known as drizzle. The official distinction between rain and drizzle is quite simple. Rain will make a splash in a puddle; drizzle will not.

Hail – In Cumulo-Nimbus cloud the up currents are so powerful that not only can very large drops be sustained but they are taken up to very great heights – often several times before leaving the cloud. At the heights they reach they freeze and fall as drops of ice called hail.

Snow – When condensation takes place below freezing point the water vapour changes directly into ice crystals. When these crystals join up and become heavy enough they fall as snow.

– A mixture of rain and snow is known as sleet.

Fog – Fog is Stratus at ground level and is a great hazard to pilots in flight. Internationally fog is said to exist when visibility falls below 1 km; but in the UK the official figure is 200 yards (180 metres) before any public warning is issued.

There are basically two types of fog:

– **Radiation Fog**

After sunset when no further heating of the earth's surface can take place, if the sky is cloudless the heat stored rapidly radiates into the atmosphere and the surface quickly cools. The air in contact with the cold surface will also cool and if the relative humidity is very high not much will be required to meet dew point and thus condensation.

In summer the longer days see the surface storing so much heat that it is not finally cool enough to cause condensation in the air until around dawn – hence early morning mists.

In winter the heat received is much less so the cooling time to dew point is much less – hence fog shortly after sunset. Radiation fog requires a light wind to trigger it off but will not form when a reasonable wind is blowing. The stronger wind mixes the air and prevents a well defined cooling at the surface with low Stratus being formed rather than fog.

– **Advection Fog**

This is caused when a warm air mass passes over a colder surface; it is particularly prevalent at sea. If such a mass moves into a region of colder sea the lower levels of the air mass are cooled and they condense into fog banks.

Fog banks normally disperse if blown inland as the warmer land evaporates the fog back into water vapour. However, if the land happens to be as cold then the fog will remain. In winter when the sea is relatively warmer than the land – particularly at night – any fog moving off the land will disperse on contact with the sea.

– If the strength of the sun is sufficient all types of fog will burn away after a time. If complete dispersal is not effected the fog may lift from the ground and remain as low Stratus.

– Fog is predictable given that one knows the temperature and relative humidity at the time.

- Great care should be taken in flying at sunset during autumn and winter when skies are clear; radiation fog can quite suddenly form and catch you napping.

Thunder – Thunderstorms occur in fully developed Cu-Nimb clouds and have the habit of fascinating people or scaring them silly – there seems to be no happy medium.

- Large water droplets can form in the vigorous upcurrents, freeze, and can equally be broken down by same, leading to them becoming positively electrified. The air becomes charged and eventually when large amounts of electricity accumulate a lightning flash occurs.

- 'Forked' lightning is the visible sign of a discharge from cloud to earth.

- 'Sheet' lightning is the discharge from cloud to cloud where the flash is diffused by the cloud.

- The noise which follows a lightning flash is set up by the sudden heating and expansion of the air followed by an equally rapid cooling and contraction.

- A rough estimate of the distance a thunderstorm is away from you is to allow a mile for every five seconds between flash and noise.

Weather is very much associated with pressure systems. Naturally the intensity of the weather will be related to the intensity of the system.

Depression (Low) – Bad weather with continuous rain, high winds and low cloud. Usually associated with fronts. Winds veer as each front passes.

Trough – Similar to a depression but not so long lasting.

Col – Neutral weather. If a high lapse rate exists with a high relative humidity there will be a tendency towards thundery conditions.

Anti-Cyclone (High) – Good weather, dry, often bringing cloudless skies in winter and summer.

- In winter the air will be colder and the relative humidity higher therefore cloud is more likely to form. This will burn away or not burn away according to the thickness of the cloud layer and the strength of the sun at the time.

- When a really thick layer exists during the quiet period of a High it gives rise to exceptional dullness known as 'Anti-cyclonic Gloom'.

- Air in a High is basically stable and no convection to speak about is usually present. This gives rise to hazy conditions in summer with the likelihood of anything from mist to thick fog in winter.

– Visibility is certainly a problem during these conditions especially when flying up sun.

Ridge – Period of settled weather between two poor spells.

Air Density and its Effect on Flight

Having covered pressure, temperature and relative humidity earlier, before closing the pages on Met we need to discuss *density*, the aspect that is not directly measurable on an instrument.

Density is the weight of the molecules in a given mass (or parcel) of air. Just as pressure decreases as you ascend, density also decreases as the air becomes thinner with height.

Density is also affected by temperature. When a parcel of air is heated it expands and the number of molecules in the original volume decreases. (Fig.39)

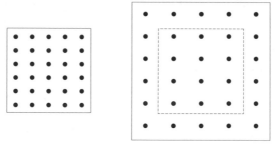

Fig. 39 Expansion on heating

The reverse takes place when air is cooled.

Density is not to be confused with pressure. The latter is the weight of a column of air up through the atmosphere from the surface.

If at a given time the air in a column is heated the air will indeed expand but in so doing it increases the length (height) of the column. The weight in the column remains the same. (Fig.40)

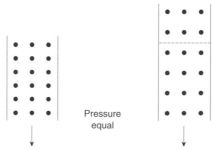

Fig. 40 The column increases – pressure remains the same in both columns.

So we now see that density decreases
- with a decrease in pressure
- with an increase in temperature.

Finally, contrary to what you may imagine, the more water vapour present in the air the less dense that air will be leading to a final conclusion that:

As relative humidity increases – density decreases.

So what effect has this on flight? If density decreases, the air passing over the wing becomes thinner and likewise the number of air molecules entering the air speed indicator (ASI) will be less than normal. The ASI reading will now reduce to below your actual speed through the air which is True Airspeed. (See page 185).

During take-off, to bring the indicated airspeed up to flying speed, for sufficient lift to permit take-off, means increasing the groundspeed. In so doing the take-off distance will now increase and there will also be a reduction in climb rate in the thinner air compared with that shown in the aircraft manual.

Performance figures shown in such manuals assume the use of a *hard* runway and are all based on the International Standard Atmosphere figures which you should use as a yardstick. When the airfield pressure is **less** than 1013.25 mbs and/or the temperature is **greater** than 15°C the air density will have **decreased**. Here is an example of the effect.

Take a *grass* airfield 500 ft AMSL with an air temperature of 25°C. The decrease in density due to the height of the airfield AMSL and the increased temperature above 15°C would increase the take-off run in still air by 60% and decrease the rate of climb by 25%.

To sum up. You have a high altitude airfield on a hot sticky day with the friction of grass instead of a smooth hard runway. These factors should make you think deeply as to whether you can get airborne from your strip and then clear any obstacles ahead on climb-out.

Summary

Meteorology can be a very complex subject but the foregoing in its relatively simplistic state should be sufficient for your immediate needs.

Apart from knowledge you may have gained through the pages just read, you should always pay due attention to the official weather forecasts and charts available not only from newspapers and TV stations but from other sources such as the aviation forecasts obtainable by phone or fax.

The final section in this chapter gives you details of the sources where such information can be obtained.

Sources of Aviation Forecasts

There are a host of various weather reports and forecasts available to you – some in plain language such as AIRMET and others in code such as a METAR and TAF.

As they can undergo amendment, or be added to in number from time to time, they are not dealt with in detail in this book. A full presentation of these sources and any codes involved is to be found in an excellent **FREE** booklet from the CAA called – **GET MET**

Copies of this free booklet can be obtained by sending an A5 size stamped addressed envelope to –

Safety Promotion, General Aviation Department, Civil Aviation Authority, Aviation House, Gatwick Airport South, West Sussex, RH6 0YR.

It is acknowledged that the modern microlight now has the capability to travel further than its predecessor of early days. Nevertheless, the journeys are still mainly from one microlight site to another. They are not necessarily to defined aerodromes used by other types of aircraft – aerodromes where the coded current weather report such as the METAR and the forecast such as the TAF are available for intending visitors.

You should at least become familiar with the existence of METARs and TAFs as you may be flying to a site not far from a reporting airfield where you decide it would be worthwhile to seek the information from same. However, in doing so take into account any hills, mountains and costal factors in the area; they can dramatically affect weather conditions between two locations only a few miles apart.

Concerning AIRMET, available by telephone, to maximise its use there is a form available known as the *Pilot's Proforma*. This form includes a chart and is laid out in the order the forecast is given over the phone. For first time users of the form there is an explanatory leaflet and user's notes; both the leaflet, notes and a supply of forms can be obtained **FREE** from AOPA, 50a Cambridge Street, London, SW1V 4QQ. Send an A4 size stamped addressed envelope. Photocopying the forms is permitted.

In **GET MET** there are telephone numbers for obtaining help when you find it difficult to understand or access the available information on direct contact with your local weather station has not been possible for some time. However, contact with a forcaster has been resumed for those requiring special information as an individual. This service currently costs £17 including VAT – payable by credit card. The fee does not cover the cost of the phone call.

It is essential you obtain a copy of **GET MET** to use in conjunction with the meteorological section in this book. Questions on the sources of aviation weather information may be asked in your meteorology examination paper. Ensure your copy is up to date; it is reviewed anually for any necessary amendments with a new edition usually available by late January. Between editions of *GET MET*, frequently check the index page relevant to the service required; also, any such changes can usually be found in an **Aeronautical Information Circular (AIC)** issued by the CAA.

ISA Data

Pressure	at MSL	1013.25 mbs
Altimeter Setting		1013.2 mbs
Temperature	at MSL	15° Celsius
Average Lapse Rate		–2°C per 1000 ft
(to 36,000 ft)		(–1.98°C to be precise)
Density		1225 grms per cubic metre

Note: With density not being measurable in the same manner as pressure or temperature. You must therefore **remember that**—

a density *decrease*

comes about with—

a pressure *decrease*

and/or—

a temperature *increase*

and/or—

a relative humidity *increase*

A density *increase* will come about when each of the above ocurrences are reversed.

Basic Flight Instruments

We now look at the use and working principles of four basic flight instruments – the altimeter, airspeed indicator, vertical speed indicator and magnetic compass. The diagrams will not necessarily represent the actual mechanism inside each one but they will give you an idea of the principles involved in their working.

The Altimeter

The altimeter is the instrument which indicates the height of the aircraft above a pre-selected surface level.

It is nothing more than a sensitive aneroid barometer as described in 'Basic Meteorology'; but in this case it is calibrated to read feet instead of millibars on the basis that 1 mb change in pressure equates to a change of 30 ft in terms of height. At the base is a knob which enables a selected pressure setting to be entered on the altimeter at any given time on the ground or in flight.

The atmospheric pressure, known as **static pressure** in this case, is fed to the instrument from an aperture set into the fuselage side so that it is at right angles to any airflow. (Fig.1)

Fig.1
Altimeter

Static
pressure

Static pressure
head aperture

Altimeter

As you can see, the altimeter can have a three-handed dial. The first and largest will indicate feet in 00s of feet; the second smaller one will show in 000s and the third and smallest with a ring on it depicts 0,000s. This format has led to mis-reading on a number of occasions so be particularly careful in your interpretations. It must be said in passing that whilst the occasional record breaker may need it, the idea of the average microlight pilot requiring a reading from the third and smallest hand certainly stretches the imagination!

Unlike the barometer at a reporting station, which is static and has a permanent correction applied to it to obtain MSL pressure, the altimeter is very much a mobile entity. It will be subjected to a number of variables which must be understood if effective and safe use is to be made of it.

Certain of the variables to be discussed are not strictly pertinent to micro-lights but they are worth noting if only to gain an awareness of what the 'other chap' has to face.

Atmospheric pressure at a given place is usually in a state of constant change. You will appreciate that the aneroid altimeter will respond to these changes and show corresponding changes in 'height' without ever moving. To cater for this situation, altimeters are fitted with a setting device which when set to the atmospheric pressure at the time will ensure that the altimeter is reading 0 feet on the ground.

For example:

Pressure is reading 1,000 millibars and the altimeter is reading 0 feet.

Pressure drops to 990 millibars. This drop of 10 mbs at 30 ft per millibar is equivalent to 300 ft.

The altimeter will read 300 ft.

Alter the setting scale to read 990 mbs and the altimeter will once more read 0 ft.

For an aircraft that has been airborne for some time there is the likelihood that a pressure change has taken place since take-off. When radio is fitted this is no problem as a new altimeter setting can be obtained from the control tower.

Extending this likelihood of a pressure change whilst airborne, it can have an effect on the flight path in relation to the ground.

For example:

Pressure setting at take-off is 1000 mbs

Altimeter reads 0 ft.

Course set for destination at 1500 ft.

Pressure at destination is 990 mbs

Altimeter, if on ground, at destination would read 300 ft.

An **actual** height of 1500 ft at destination would read 1,800 ft on the altimeter.

Pilot notices height 'increasing' on route and descends to keep at 1500 ft on the altimeter.

Result – a **sloping** flight path towards destination.

Actual height on arrival is 1500 ft less 300 ft due to pressure change = 1200 ft.

It needs no imagination to realise that any flight path that slopes down-wards can pose serious problems to a pilot flying 'blind' on instruments.

There may well be an obstruction on route which it is known will be avoided when flying at the planned height but would certainly be struck on an unplanned sloping flight path. (Fig.2)

Fig.2

The example on the pressure change has pre-supposed the departure and destination airfields to be at the same height. You will appreciate that in practice this will rarely be the case.

In the last example had the destination been at 300 ft above the departure then the actual height on arrival would have been 900 ft.

Altimeter Settings

It is obvious that safe flight for those having to rely on instruments demands constant contact with the ground to ensure up to date receipt of altimeter settings that not only cover atmospheric changes but also the difference that will be caused by different airfield levels.

There are four settings with which you should concern yourself. Although the fourth is mainly for IFR flights you need to know of it when in proximity to controlled airspace.

QFE   Pressure at airfield level.
Used when in proximity of home or destination airfield.
Reading from this setting is referred to as **Height**.

QNH   Pressure correct to MSL.
Used mainly on routes below 3000 ft.
Reading from this setting is referred to as **Altitude**.

Regional QNH The UK is divided into a number of regions wherein the QNH is updated for that region throughout the day at regular intervals. Such a region is known as an **Altimeter Setting Region (ASR)** and is marked on aviation charts.

Standard   The standard setting is that laid down in the ISA definition and is used when flight takes place above 3000 ft or the transition level in being at the time. When using this setting, the altimeter reading at a reporting point would be reported to ATC as a **Flight level** based on 00's of feet. For example, 15,500 ft would be FL155.
The standard setting is 1013.2MBS – the altimeter scale would not cater for the defined figure of 1013.25.

It is important that you should realise that the height of the 1013.2 pressure level can vary enormously with pressure changes in the atmosphere. For example, FL45 may not necessarily be at 4500 feet above the ground; with an actual QNH of 993.2, the designated FL45 on your chart would be only 3900 feet above the surface. So, approach this area at say 4000 feet on the QNH and you could soon end up where you should not be!

As a rough guide, when the QNH is less than 1013.2, the FL will be lower than its figure depicts.

Absence of Pressure Setting Facility

In microlight flying, altimeters are sometimes used which have no pressure setting scale.

There are two basic criteria in cross-country flying which the lack of this facility may make it difficult to satisfy at first sight. They are:
– The need for flying on QNH for terrain clearance on route.
– The need for being on QFE overhead your destination in order to join circuit at the correct height.

The answer lies in compromise. Prior to take-off, adjust the altimeter to read the height of your departure point AMSL (QNH). As you proceed across country you will at least be flying as near to QNH as you can having made this adjustment.

On arrival overhead your destination or within the immediate vicinity of it **reduce** your altimeter reading by the height AMSL of that destination point as printed on your aeronautical map.

On touch down your altimeter should now read '0' which is what you require.

An example:

Your departure point is 550 ft AMSL and your destination is 160 ft AMSL.

On route there is high ground to be cleared at 800 ft so you plan to fly at 1800 ft to give the high ground a wide berth.

Set your altimeter to read 550 ft (QNH). After take-off, a climb of 1250 ft will see you at your cruising altitude of 1800 ft.

On arrival overhead your destination, reduce your altimeter reading by 160 ft (destination height AMSL) to read 1640 ft. Your altimeter will now be reading your height above the aerodrome (QFE).

Airspeed Indicator (ASI)

The ASI, as it is usually called, does just what its name implies – tells you your speed through the air but not over the ground as you will see in the next chapter on 'Navigation'.

Quite simply, oncoming air in flight enters a forward-facing aperture on the aircraft known as the pitot tube. It is carried through a line to a capsule in the instrument which can expand or contract. The pressure this air exerts on the capsule is a combination of static pressure (already there) and the additional pressure attributed to the moving air, known as **dynamic pressure**. The effect of these two pressures is called the **total pressure**.

There is a need to ensure the capsule, and thereby the reading, is only influenced by *dynamic* pressure – the moving air. To this end, a static pressure line is also introduced into this instrument which exerts itself on the *outside* of the capsule.

This nullifies the static pressure content of the total pressure *inside* the capsule. The nett effect is that in the end only the required dynamic pressure is linked from the capsule to the dial where it is registered in terms of **statute miles** per hour **(mph)** or **nautical miles** per hour which are **knots (kts)**. (Fig.3)

Fig.3
Airspeed Indicator (ASI)

Pitot tube

Total pressure

Static pressure head aperture

The Airspeed Indicator (ASI)

A reading on an ASI is known as the **Indicated Airspeed** and can be subject to a number of effects; positioning, altitude and temperature.

Positioning – Should the pitot head be out of line with the airflow or subject to disruption by part of the aircraft structure the dynamic pressure will be distorted.

Similar distortion can occur when the line from the pitot head is 'kinked' by a fastener or too sharp a bend on its route to the ASI.

Altitude – At high level the density of the atmosphere is far less than at sea level. This will result in an overall reduction of both dynamic and static pressure.

But although the dynamic pressure in the capsule may now be less, its expansion will not decrease because the static pressure opposing it will also be less. The indicated airspeed thus remains constant.

However, the aircraft, in passing through less dense air, will be moving faster than the indicated speed for the same power due to it meeting with less resistance.

Temperature – Temperature can have an effect on density at all levels and therefore have an effect on both dynamic and static pressure.

Pilots who need to fly on instruments alone, with no means of relating to the ground for visual position checks, can deal with the last two problems by use of a navigation computer which enables indicated airspeed to be converted into **True Airspeed**.

∗ There is a stage between indicated and true airspeed known as **Rectified Airspeed** where any correction for a particular instrument appears on a card in the cockpit.∗∗

An example of a navigational computer can be found in the chapter on 'Navigation' and it would do no harm for the microlight pilot to practise the use of same using the instruction booklet.

Vertical Speed Indicator (VSI)

The VSI indicates the rate at which an aircraft is climbing or descending in terms of feet per minute. Once again we have a capsule capable of expansion/contraction in the operation of this instrument; this time it is related to the speed at which pressure decreases or increases on climb or descent.

In this case static pressure has instant entry/exit to the capsule but its entry/exit to the area surrounding the capsule is only gradual due to the other aperture being restricted to deliberately delay movement either way. (Fig.4)

Instant entry/exit   Gradual entry/exit   **Fig.4**

The Vertical Speed Indicator (VSI)

In level flight the pressure both inside and outside the capsule will be the same so the instrument will show a zero reading.

The operation in climb and descent is as follows:

Climb – Pressure in the capsule decreases as air *instantly* exits into the lower atmospheric pressure outside. Pressure on the capsule is now temporarily greater due to the pin-hole aperture allowing only a *gradual* exit of the air around it into the atmosphere.

The capsule therefore contracts under the greater pressure and the contraction is registered on the dial as rate of ascent.

Descent – Pressure in the capsule increases as air *instantly* enters the capsule from the higher atmospheric pressure outside.

Pressure on the capsule is temporarily less due to the pin-hole aperture allowing only a *gradual* entry of air into the capsule's surround.

The capsule therefore expands and the expansion is registered on the dial as rate of descent.

There is a minor problem with this instrument which calls for anticipation developed with practice. When the aircraft levels out after climb or descent, the delay caused by the gradual entry/exit of air through the pin-hole aperture will continue to register a rate of climb/descent on the dial until pressure in the instrument has equalised with that in the capsule. At this time, when you have levelled out, pay attention to the altimeter otherwise you can end up 'chasing the VSI' in oscillating flight.

You may be wondering why, in the case of all the instruments covered, the static pressure line is fed to the exterior of the aircraft – why not just a hole in the instrument you may say?

The reason is simple. Should the instrument be housed in a heated cabin this will lead to a decrease in air density in turn leading to a reduced pressure reading.

Altimeter, ASI and VSI Problems

The three instruments just discussed have one factor in common – they all rely on static pressure. With the relatively limited entry aperture on the static pressure line in terms of size it is very susceptible to blockage by the smallest particles of matter. Should this happen you could end up with false readings; static pressure inside the instrument will now be fixed and invariably differ from static pressure inside a capsule.

Icing can also be a problem when super-cooled liquid drops are ingested and freeze.

To enable these two possibilities to be overcome, many aircraft have an alternative interior static inlet. When necessary the line is switched to this internal aperture and allowance is then made for the effect of a lesser static pressure element.

Perhaps it should be pointed out that such a nicety as an alternative static pressure inlet is unlikely to be found on many microlight aeroplanes – if any.

The ASI has an added problem with the dynamic pressure inlet in the form of the pitot tube having a much larger aperture. Not only can it pick up larger particles of matter in the air but it is also an excellent collector of rubbish on the ground thrown up by such as another aircraft running up in front of you or in close proximity.

This is overcome by the fitting of a sleeve cover over the pitot head at all times when the machine is not in use. But do make sure it is removed during your pre-flight check; fail to do so and you will have become one of many members of an elite (?) club of pilots who have had the wind up them instead of through the pitot tube!

Again, because the pitot tube faces directly into the airflow it can ingest much more water in flight to encourage freezing – given that icing conditions exist. The latter problem is solved on many aeroplanes by fitting a heated pitot head around the tube; but again, not likely to be found on microlights.

One final point; *never, ever*, blow into a pitot tube to check that an ASI is working – after doing so it probably won't!

The Magnetic Compass

The magnetic compass is well known to most people be they aviators or not. The magnetic field around the Earth converges on points close to the north and south geographic poles called the Northern and Southern **Magnetic Poles (NMP** and **SMP)**. Hence, a magnetised bar will always tend to point towards the NMP.

This principle enables the heading of an aircraft to be read off by a pilot against a fixed lubber line set against a needle or card linked to the magnetised bar. The readings will normally show N, S, E and W with the intervals between marked for each 30 degrees. Further sub-divisions between the 30 degree marks are shown for every 5 degrees. (Fig.5)

Fig.5
Magnetic Compass

Lubber
line

＊ To an aircraft in the air, the compass needle not only tends towards north but it will also tend downwards towards the NMP deep within the Earth until theoretically it would point vertically down when directly over it. This effect is known as magnet dip and, if fixed to its pivot point, the bar would jam up long before it reached such an extreme. (Fig.6)

Fig.6
Magnet Dip

MAGNETIC DIP

At the Equator the bar would remain horizontal, being under the influence of both NMP and SMP, but progress towards northern or southern latitudes will see the dip increase. To reduce this natural effect to a practical minimum, the bar is not fixed to its pivot point but is suspended from it. It now has the free movement of a pendulum in any direction.

By adopting this method of suspension, as dip takes place the centre of gravity (CG) of the bar is displaced; the weight now becomes offset from the pivot point and acts against the dip effect. This counter-action is sufficient to limit dip to a mere few degrees of no consequence. (Fig.7)

DIP CONTROL

Fig.7
Dip Control

The weight is now offset from the pivot point thus resisting the dip effect and preventing it becoming excessive

So much for the workings of the magnetic compass. ＊＊

Compass Problems

As with all instruments the magnetic compass has its own foibles of which you need to be aware, even if the reason escapes you or is never fully understood. There are times in flight when you can increase or decrease speed and notice a change in the indicated heading taking place without any sort of a turn having been initiated.

The same effect can be experienced in a turn when on rolling out of same on to your new heading, the compass goes on moving or else begins to reverse direction. In short, these effects can come about whenever you take your aircraft out of equilibrium (constant speed/height/heading).

With the former there is no need to do anything; the heading will revert back to normal when the aircraft settles down to its new speed – that is when equilibrium is restored. In the latter case remedial action can be taken to prevent you over or under correcting.

* What causes all this to happen? The effects stem from the pendulum set-up, geared to prevent dip, which allows the CG of the magnetic bar to roam, for the want of a better word. This is just what it does as acceleration or deceleration takes place when an increase or decrease in speed is initiated.

Flying directly along a north/south line will show no change as the CG movement will be along this axis. However, flying from west to east or vice-versa then the offset CG counteracting dip will hang back in acceleration and move forward on deceleration. This causes the compass reading to deviate from the required heading until, as already said, equilibrium is restored. (Fig.8)

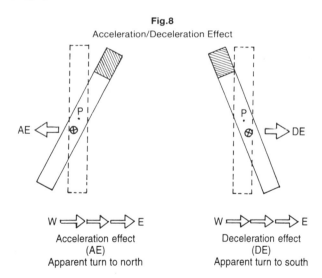

Fig.8
Acceleration/Deceleration Effect

AE

DE

W ⟹⟹⟹ E
Acceleration effect
(AE)
Apparent turn to north

W ⟹⟹⟹ E
Deceleration effect
(DE)
Apparent turn to south

When a turn is initiated another form of acceleration force (centripetal) is set up towards the centre of that turn. It is apart from any force introduced by a change in speed and this also adds to the problem of wandering headings due to the pendulum format of the bar. You can come out of a turn and find the compass reading under or over that required; in other words the needle is under or over shooting the lubber line. You should now appreciate that with changes in speed or direction there is an almost infinite number of permutations where the heading can stray from that required and the degree to which it may do so. **

In a nutshell where the turn is concerned it means that on rolling out of the turn when your compass reaches the required new heading, you must anticipate the afore-mentioned effects. This is achieved by timing the manoeuvre just right to ensure the compass stops on the desired heading without repeated correction moves having to be made.

The degree to which these effects take place is governed by whether you are heading in an overall northerly or southerly direction when the turn is initiated.

The following table will give you a broad indication of what to do in a turn.

Northerly – Roll-out is made early
Southerly – Roll-out is made late

For example:

Initial Hdg.	New Hdg.	Roll-out	
280	030	at 010	(early)
030	280	300	(early)
220	140	120	(late)
140	220	240	(late)

Finally, in the next chapter which deals with 'Navigation' and the *use* you make of compass readings, you will learn about the effect of deviation. This is caused through magnetic fields created by aircraft themselves. Deviation is peculiar to each individual aircraft and the corrections calibrated should be visible in the cockpit on a deviation card. A new card is essential if any modifications are carried out, particularly when the changes or additions are made to electrical equipment.

Again, beware of any *additional* items of a metallic or electrical nature inadvertently placed near the compass during flight. Such items could be keyrings, transistor radios, mobile phones, metal map boards and so forth. They can contribute to errors in readings for which the deviation card has not allowed.

There are many more flight instruments we could discuss but they are mostly slanted towards blind flying in clouds or flight in keeping with IFR which is not part of the microlight scene.

Navigation

Introduction

Navigation and map reading are often associated with each other in aviation text books. However, in this book the accent is on microlight aeroplanes and navigation may be considered by pilots of same to be irrelevant.

"There is no way I can plot on charts when exposed to a 50 to 60 mph airstream rushing past" – is often the natural retort to the suggestion of navigation under these circumstances.

Because of the limitations imposed by microlight flight the two subjects must be looked at thus:

NAVIGATION – is PLANNING your way from A to B prior to flight.

MAP READING – is FINDING your way from A to B during flight.

With regard to the former, the serious navigator uses charts devoid of all detail other than the lines of latitude and longitude and certain major features. There is therefore plenty of room for pencilled plots and calculations all of which will be clearly legible.

In a microlight, plotting charts will never enter the picture – basically you will find yourself confined to the use of aeronautical maps and with the wealth of detail thereon little room will be found for anything but the barest of calculations.

In actual fact you will find that any calculations you may choose to make can be quite easily carried out on a sheet of plain paper.

Global Positioning System (GPS)

One piece of advice. Vast advances in technology linked to satellites have made available the most compact forms of navigational aids to get you effortlessly to your destination.

A slim box about the size of a pocket calculator can tell you precisely the direction to go, how far it is to your destination, how long it will take you to get there and finally it will tell you when you are there – within a matter of yards.

It is affordable and therefore attractive; *but* rely on it in place of a prepared flight plan worked out from a sound basic knowledge of navigation and you do so at your peril. Ask those who chose the easy option what happened when the batteries ran out in flight!

Think of GPS as 'Global Positioning Second'; first comes your own basic flight planning and an up to date aeronautical chart – clearly marked with your intended track. The second is indeed first class but must ever remain only a back-up.

Position Plot

Establishing your position on a map or chart is a natural pre-requisite for navigating.

The earth is divided up into segments by lines of latitude and longitude which run as follows:

Latitude – Lines at 1° intervals running parallel to the north and south of the Equator ranging from 0° to 90° N. or S.

Longitude – Lines at 1° intervals running east and west of a line running from the North to the South Pole which passes through Greenwich. This base line is known as the Greenwich Meridian and longitude is measured in a range of 0° to 180° E. or W. of Greenwich. (See Fig.1)

Degrees of latitude and longitude are broken down into 'minutes' with 60 minutes equal to 1 degree.

A position can therefore be given for any place in the world expressed as degrees/minutes north or south of the Equator and east or west of the Greenwich Meridian.

In terms of distance, 1 minute is equal to 1 Nautical Mile (NM) which in turn is equal to one and one seventh statute miles along lines of latitude.

Where longitude is concerned a minute can only equal 1 nm along the Equator. North or south of this latitude the lines of longitude converge on the poles progressively narrowing as they do so.

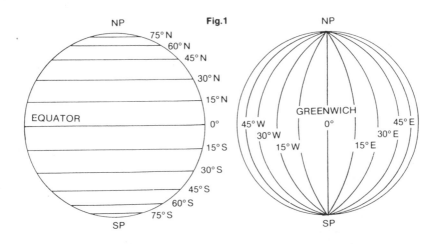

Fig.1

Compass Readings

Compass readings are in degrees from 001° to 360°.

There is a discrepancy between the geographical north (**True North**) and the direction in which a compass needle will point (**Magnetic North**). The angle is known as **Variation**. This angle can vary both with time and with position on the Earth's surface. Lines joining places of equal variation are known as **Isogonals** – they will be shown on your maps in terms of amount and the date will be that pertaining to the map itself.

A further complication is caused by magnetic fields created by aircraft themselves as described in the previous chapter. The further difference between the magnetic north and the direction in which the compass needle points (**Compass North**) is the angle known as **Deviation**.

In navigation all bearings or headings are related to **True North** (the Geographical North) so to establish a **Compass Heading – Hdg.(C)** which will provide a required **True Heading – Hdg.(T)** there are a few minor calculations to be made.

Variation and deviation can be either east or west, a situation which can be confusing unless some form of 'jingle' is remembered to help avoid mistakes. It is this:

'Variation West – Magnetic Best' – Add to True Heading

'Variation East – Magnetic Least' – Subtract from True Heading.

The same jingle applies to deviation but for 'magnetic' read 'compass'. Remember, variation is applied to **True** headings and deviation to **Magnetic** headings. Examples can be found in Fig.2.

(Note symbols for types of North)

Other examples:

Fig.2

The following are some examples for you to work out.

	Hdg.(T)	Var.	Hdg.(M)	Dev.	Hdg.(C)
(i)	102°	10°W		3°E	
(ii)	224°	8°W		2°W	
(iii)	049°	5°E		1°W	
(iv)		3°W		2°E	164°
(v)		6°E	331°	4°W	
(vi)	140°		145°		143°

(The answers may be found at the end of the chapter).

Navigational Instruments

A limited number of simple instruments are required for solving navigational problems 'by hand' for the want of a better term.

Protractor — For measuring headings against lines of longitude.

Navigational Rule — For measuring distance in nautical or statute miles. The scale of the rule must match that of the map. An ordinary ruler used in conjunction with the scale on the map will suffice if nothing else is to hand.

Dividers/Compasses — For transporting measurements from the rule on to your working.

Manual and electronic computers are available for carrying out all navigational problems – their use is a matter of personal choice. Learning to use them is best undertaken by working out examples on the computers themselves as per the makers instructions rather than attempting to follow diagrams in a book. Also, you could well have to work out answers for yourself in any examination you may take so reliance on mechanical or electronic aids is not such a good thing.

Track and Heading

The line drawn on your map depicting your route from A to B is known as the **Track Required (Tr.Req)**.

By measuring the angle of the track in relation to a line of longitude you establish the direction you must travel in relation to True North. This direction is known as your **True Heading (Hdg.T)** and to this must be applied Variation to establish your **Magnetic Heading (Hdg.)** to ensure that your travel will be along the Tr.Req. in relation to True North.

Deviation must be applied where necessary but as this alters from aircraft to aircraft and also with the direction in which the aircraft happens to be heading we will from this moment on take it as read and ignore it for the purposes of demonstrating problems.

Timing

If you know the **Airspeed** at which you are going to fly and you know the distance along your track then it is possible to lay down the time your flight will take thus allowing you to state an **Estimated Time of Arrival (ETA)** based on your actual time of departure.

The formula is quite simply: $$\frac{\text{Distance of Track}}{\text{Airspeed}}$$

ensuring that both inputs are in the same terminology viz. nautical miles or statute miles. Take great care in working out problems to make sure that you never mix the two.

All this is fine in still air but rarely will you come across such conditions and this is where your problems begin.

Effect of Wind

Referring back for a moment to the effect of wind on take-off and landing you will recall that your airspeed for sustaining flight was reached at a lower groundspeed when pointing into wind. Fine for achieving take-off in the shortest possible distance but a factor to be reckoned with once airborne and wanting to reach your destination in the quickest possible time.

For example, take Fig.3

Fig.3

HEADWIND

W/S 15 MPH
RESULTING G/S 30 MPH

A/S 45 MPH

On a trip of 90 miles at an airspeed of 45 mph the flight time in still air would be two hours. However, as in Fig.3 with the headwind reducing your actual **Groundspeed** to 30 mph the time in air will turn out to be 3 hours.

Should your planned fuel allow for 2½ hours time in air you can see that because of the headwind you will in fact be back on the ground after covering only 75 miles with 15 miles unattained – assuming a 30 mph groundspeed.

Conversely, a tailwind will add to groundspeed for a given airspeed. In the example given, at an airspeed of 45 mph the groundspeed will be 60 mph thus seeing your 90 mile track being covered in 1½ hours leaving plenty of fuel to spare.

To complicate matters further, just as still air is something of a rarity so is the likelihood of your **Track Required (Tr.Req.)** being precisely upwind or downwind.

Triangle of Velocities

Returning to the water again. A boat intends to cross a river from A to B which is the Tr.Req. However, a current is flowing which will make the boat track from A to C when the heading is set towards B. This resulting track is known as the **Track Made Good (TMG)**.

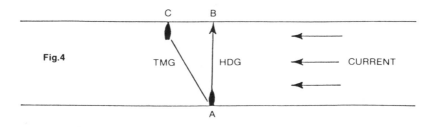

Fig.4

TMG   HDG   CURRENT

To counteract the current and ensure that the TMG coincides with the Tr.Req. means adopting a **Heading** into the current. If the adjustment is not correct then the *angle* between TMG and Tr.Req. is known as **Track Error**. The angle between heading and TMG is called **Drift**.

Fig.5

In the air a similar adjustment must be made to counteract any drift caused by the wind. This adjustment will always be **into** the windward side of the track.

The exact amount of adjustment is calculated by drawing three **Vectors** to form a **Triangle of Velocities**.

Each vector comprises a velocity related to the flight – a velocity being a speed and a direction.

The three velocities are—

(i) True Heading – Hdg.(T) – The direction the aircraft is pointing in relation to True North.

True Airspeed – TAS – The indicated airspeed corrected for instrument error, temperature and altitude in mph or knots – a knot being 1 nm per hour.

(ii) Wind Direction – W – The direction **from** which the wind blows in relation to True North.

Wind Speed – V – Speed in mph or knots

(iii) Track Required – Tr.Req. – The direction the aircraft is required to travel over the ground in relation to True North.

Groundspeed – GS – The speed at which the aircraft travels along the track in relation to the ground – in mph or knots.

Given any two of the above vectors the third can always be deduced.
We will now take an example and follow it through

You wish to go from A to B.   The two unknowns are:
Distance is 60 statute miles   Hdg.(T) to counter Drift.
Tr.Req. is 215° (T)   GS resulting from wind effect.
Wind (W/V) is 140°/15 mph
TAS will be 50 mph.

- With a protractor and a ruler, use a longitude line on your map (or a vertical line on plain paper as per the example) and lay off a line from A to B at 215° True North – the Tr.Req. Mark this line with two arrows. (Fig.6a)
- Next lay off a wind line at 140° *downwind* from start point A. Mark this line with three arrows. Now select a scale which is large enough to allow accuracy and small enough to allow your protractor to be used as dividers. To depict the 15 mph wind vector, measure off the dividers to 15 on your scale and outward from A along the wind line intersect with an arc X.1. (Fig.6b)
- Next, to depict the 50 mph TAS vector, measure off the dividers to 50 and out from X.1 intersect the A to B line with an arc X.2 and mark this line with one arrow. The length of line from **A to X.2** shows the actual GS will be 44 mph due to the part headwind. (Fig. 6c)
- Finally, extend the line back from X.2 to X.1 to intersect the True North (vertical) line at X.3. The **angle of the line** related to True North will give you a Hdg.T. of 198° needed to keep the Tr.Req. (Fig 6d)
- You have now calculated the two unknowns GS and Hdg – the former one shows that your 60 mile journey at 44 mph will take 82 minutes. Working in entirety is shown in Fig.6e.

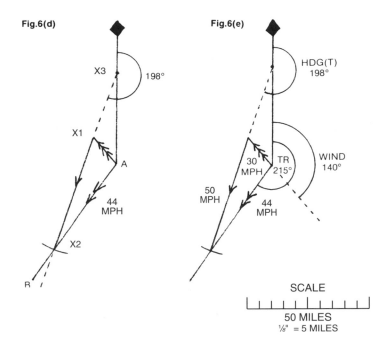

Fig.6(d)

X3   198°

X1

A

44
MPH

X2

B

Fig.6(e)

HDG(T)
198°

30
MPH   TR
215°   WIND
140°

50
MPH

44
MPH

SCALE

| | | | | | | | | | | |
50 MILES
⅛" = 5 MILES

A few points to remember about the Triangle of Velocities.

– Again, speed in mph or knots is immaterial as long as they are not mixed in any one calculation.

– The heading and wind arrows should always be following each other around the triangle and be in opposition to the track arrows.

– Think about what you are doing. Try to visualise the way the vectors should be pointing as you consider the problem. For example, in the problem just discussed (Fig.6) the wind had a lot of 'head' component in it so obviously GS should work out to be **less** than TAS.

Also, the Hdg.(T) should obviously be **less** than the Tr.Req. by virtue of the rule that adjustment is always **into** wind of track.

– When winds are directly head on or tail on to Tr.Req., no triangle is necessary – you simply subtract or add on the windspeed to the TAS to read GS.

A Reciprocal Track

There will be occasions when your flight is an 'out and return'. In other words the flight home will cover the same ground as the outward path – known as a reciprocal. The reciprocal track will therefore be the outward Tr.Req. plus or minus 180°.

The heading for home is not so straightforward to work out; setting this up means you must again take any drift into account. To prevent a mistake it is safer to work out a new triangle of velocities; however, there is an alternative method. Given wind velocity has not changed, you will find that the heading you require is the *reciprocal of your outward heading* (not track) less *double the drift* experienced on the outward journey.

For example, your outward track was 280° but the heading was 295° to counteract drift of 15° to port. The heading home for the reciprocal Tr.Req. will therefore be 296 – 180 = 115° less (15° x 2) = 085°.

By now you should be able to produce vectors, so prove this point for yourself diagrammatically – it will be good practice anyway.

The Navigational Computer

For those of you seeking an easy way to solve triangle of velocities problems you cannot do better than arm yourself with an Airtour CRP-1 Computer.

This particular model can be scaled down to microlight flying speeds, providing you do not intend to fly in winds over 24 knots, yet it still retains the capability of working out a host of other flight calculations.

Before delving into what it can do, let us familiarise ourselves with the main parts of the computer itself. (Fig.7)
Pay particular attention to the speed arcs and drift lines.

The speed arcs are the parallel curves across the slide and the figures from 10 to 120 running up the centre are the speed values of those arcs in knots or miles per hour – whichever you choose. Use either knots or mph but again never mix the two.

The drift lines running up the slide fan out, and as they do so the figures to be found on them – to the left and right of the centre line – represent degrees of drift.

Each sub-division of speed arc and drift line is valued at 2.

Now to some of the problems and the ways in which they can be solved. Naturally you will need to have an Airtour CRP-1 in your hand for the following to be meaningful. Use the 'ML' slide throughout.

To Set up Wind Velocity (W/V)

Method:
– The first step is understanding how to represent wind speed on the computer.
– This is set up by selecting a datum point on the centre line and pencilling in on the window a dot (or cross) **upwards** from this datum to the value of the wind speed.

Fig.7

– For example, if the 40 speed arc is used as a datum and the wind speed is 20, then the wind dot or cross would be placed on the 60 speed arc.

– In fact it is suggested you use 40 as the datum for all calculations.

– Remember, when you see W/V expressed as say 260/15 it means the wind direction is 260°(T) and the speed 15 knots or mph according to which measurement of speed you intend to use.

Now for an example—

Problem: Set up a W/V of 260/15

Solution: – Set the wind direction of 260° on the rotating scale against the index point on the outer fixed scale.

Using 40 as a datum, pencil in the 15 wind speed over the 55 speed arc (40 + 15 = 55).

Now we can begin to solve other problems.

To find True Heading (Hdg T) and Ground Speed (GS) given W/V, Track Required (Tr.Req.) and True Airspeed (TAS)

Method:

– Set up the given W/V
– Set Tr.Req. on rotating scale against index point
– Move the slide until the wind dot is over the TAS speed arc
– Under the centre point, read off the GS.
– Note the drift line value under the wind dot – either port or starboard.
– Under this drift value figure on the port or starboard side of the fixed scale as appropriate, read off the Hdg (T) on the rotating scale.

Again, an example—

Problem: Find Hdg (T) and GS when W/V is 330/20, Tr.Req. is 045° (T) and TAS is 50.

Solution: – Set up W/V of 330/20
– Set Tr.Req. of 045 against index point
– Move the slide until wind dot is over the 50 speed arc
– Under centre point read off the GS 41
– Drift value under wind dot is 24°
– Under 24° of drift on fixed scale, read off Hdg (T) or 021°T on rotating scale.

Now let us reverse the problem.

To Find Track (TR) and GS Given W/V, Hdg (T) and TAS

Method:

– Set up the W/V but with wind dot **downwards** from datum point
– Set Hdg (T) on rotating scale against index point
– Move the slide until the centre point is over the TAS speed arc
– Under the wind dot, read off GS
– Note the drift line value under the wind dot – either port or starboard
– Under the drift value figure on the fixed scale read off the Tr. on the rotating scale.

So:-

Problem: Find Tr. and GS when W/V is 330/20, Hdg (T) is 021°(T) and TAS is 50

Solution: – Set up W/V of 330/20 (with V **down** from Datum)
– Set Hdg (T) of 021° (T) against index point
– Move the slide until the centre point is over TAS 50
– Under the wind dot, read off GS 41
– Drift value under wind dot is 24°
– Under 24° of drift on fixed scale, read off Tr. of 045° (T) on rotating scale.

Next–

To Find W/V Given Tr (T), Hdg (T), GS and TAS

Method:
- Set Tr. on rotating scale against index mark
- Move the slide until the centre point is over the GS speed arc
- Note the difference in degrees to left or right of Hdg(T) in relation to Tr. which will of course be degrees of drift to port or starboard
- Pencil in wind dot over point where the drift value line just assessed crosses the TAS speed arc
- Rotate the scale until wind dot is on centre line **upwards** from the centre point.
- Against index point, read off wind direction
- The wind speed value is that measured from centre point to wind dot or, more briefly
- Read off W/V on centre line.

Thus:-

Problem: Find W/V when Tr is 045° (T), Hdg (T) is 021° (T), TAS is 50 and GS is 41.

Solution: – Set Ta 045° Ts against index
             – Set centre point over GS 41
             – Hdg (T) is 24° to port of Tr
             – Mark dot on 24° port drift line above TAS 50
             – Rotate scale until wind dot is **Upwards** from centre
             – Point on centre line
             – Read off W/V on centre line 330/20

Taking the reverse side of the Airtour CRP-1 you can ask yourself:

What is my speed in knots as mph?

What is my poundage all-up-weight in kilos?

How much fuel do I need?

How long can I stay up?

What speed do I need to cover X miles in Y minutes?

What is my speed as a Mach No!!

The latter question may be slightly academic as far as a microlight is concerned but it is indicative of the range of problems that can be solved. In fact the range is far too extensive to cover in detail in this book. In any case, using the instructions and working out your own examples is by far the best way of familiarising yourself with its operation.

Broadly speaking the outer fixed and inner rotating scales both combine to form a circular slide rule capable of simple multiplication and division apart from the specialist tasks it can undertake. (Fig.8)

Those of you with the slightest experience of flying in the average micro-light will have realised that the second and third problems would be difficult to solve as they require working out whilst airborne and computers can make short work of propellers!

However, who knows what the future holds? Maybe you could one day find yourself as navigator in a two-seat enclosed cockpit so be prepared.

Fig.8

The 1-in-60 RULE

The 1-in-60 Rule

Your flight plan prepared on the ground is not working out in the air.

– The Met man was wrong in the winds he gave you.
– You forgot to adjust for variation or deviation.
– You are not flying at the planned airspeed.
– Your compass is out.

The result is that with all your planning you end up having travelled a Track Made Good (TMG) which is not the Tr.Req. Recalculating whilst alone in a microlight exposed to the elements is not very feasible but if you can put up with a modicum of mental arithmetic then help is at hand. The 1-in-60 rule is a better than nothing way to put things right in spite of limitations.

The rule is based on the principle that for every 1 mile off track after travelling 60 miles you will have been 1° out in your heading – there will have been 1° of drift or **Track Error** which is the term used to describe the difference between TMG and Tr.Req.

$$\text{Thus, Track Error} = \frac{\text{Distance off Track} \times 60}{\text{Distance Gone}} \text{ or } \frac{\text{DOT} \times 60}{\text{DG}}$$

E.g. On a journey of 100 miles you find yourself 6 miles to starboard of Tr.Req. at point B after travelling 40 miles.

$$\text{Track Error} = \frac{6 \times 60}{40} = 9° \text{ Starboard}$$

Adjusting your heading by 9° to **Port** will stop the drift but leave you on a track parallel to Tr.Req. As your waypoints relate to Tr.Req. it is essential to regain your original track as soon as possible.

The rule is to **double** your track error – in this case making it 18° to port and this will see your Tr.Req. regained at point C in the same time it took to reach point B.

Remember that on regaining your Tr.Req. you must adjust your heading again by the original track error, that is, 9° Stbd and this will ensure that you maintain Tr.Req. from then on.

This rule also provides you with a time check as well as visual checks to help you establish Tr.Req. once again.

The formula to regain Tr.Req. thus becomes

$$\frac{2 \times \text{Distance off Track} \times 60}{\text{Distance gone}} \text{ or } \frac{2 \times \text{DOT} \times 60}{\text{DG}}$$

Fig.9

All simple rules have their limitations and the 1-in-60 Rule is no exception. After you have reached the half way mark of your flight applying the rule will see you regain your original track but **after** your destination has passed.

Some recommend that in this instance you triple your track error and in certain circumstances this works.

A more useful approach at this stage in the flight – certainly if two thirds of it have passed – would be to adjust your heading so that you reach your destination. This would avoid 'zig-zagging' which would result in the alternative of adjusting to regain Tr.Req.

To do this the formula is $\dfrac{\text{DOT} \times 60 \times \text{Total Track}}{\text{DG} \qquad \text{Dist.to go}}$ or $\dfrac{\text{DOT} \times 60 \times \text{TTr}}{\text{DG} \qquad \text{DTG}}$

E.g. On the 100 mile track you are 6 miles to starboard off that track after travelling 60 miles

Adjustment to Destination $\dfrac{\text{DOT} \times 60 \times \text{TTr}}{\text{DG} \qquad \text{DTG}} = \dfrac{6 \times 60 \times 100}{60 \qquad 40} = 15°$ Port

Fig.10

Now for the limitations. Any distance off Tr.Req. means that the 'Distance to Go' will be greater than the simple deduction of 'Distance Gone' from Total Track.

However this discrepancy only becomes a real problem when the DOT is considerable and adjustment is left until the latter stages of the journey. In the above example use of a protractor will show that the adjustment should in fact be around 14° to port – this is because the 'Distance to Go' is in reality just over 42 miles.

The 1-in-60 Rule and its uses can only be of partial help but certainly for adjustments made early in the flight – when they should be made – it can be most accurate. Try checking with a ruler and a protractor and you will be surprised at the accuracy.

The 10° Method

If you are averse to mental calculations there is another method you can use for heading corrections based on pure estimation on your part.

On your map draw lines at 10° to either side of your Tr.Req. line from the starting point and from the destination. (Fig.11)

Fig.11

Suppose after a time you realise that you are off track and your position is pinpointed as X.

By simply making an educated estimate you can see this position X to be about 7° to starboard of your Tr.Req. (Fig.12)

Fig.12

A change in heading of 7° to port will simply result in a track from X parallel to the Tr.Req.

However, you can also see that X is around 5° off Tr.Req. when related to the 10° line coming **from** the destination.

Add the two bearings together (7° + 5°) and an alteration in heading of 12° to port will see you safely to your destination.

General Data

I.A.S. – Indicated Airspeed – As shown on the airspeed indicator (A.S.I.) sufficient for microlight flying.

T.A.S. – True Airspeed – The airspeed corrected for outside air temperature (O.A.T.) using a computer.

Answers to Exercises on Page 194

(i)	112° (M)	109° (C)
(ii)	232° (M)	234° (C)
(iii)	044° (M)	045° (C)
(iv)	163° (T)	166° (M)
(v)	337° (T)	335° (C)
(vi)	5° (W)	2° (E)

Map Reading

Mastering the art of map reading is largely a matter of practice allied to knowing a few basics – a case of doing with the minimum amount of learning. Most of the latter will come from frequent study of the legend found at the foot of every map. So possession and study of the relevant maps is a far better way of learning than reading a book where becoming familiar with symbols is concerned.

Maps Available

There are two main scales used in UK light aviation covering various regions of the country. They are—
- The ¼ Million   –   Scale 1:250,000   –   4 st. mls to 1" approx.
- The ½ Million   –   Scale 1:500,000   –   8 st. mls to 1" approx.

The ¼ Million is able to show much more detail and at the speed and height a microlight aircraft travels there is time to absorb this detail. However, on the longer type of journey at above say 2,000 ft. the ½ Million with detail limited to major features would prove quite adequate and would also reduce the number of maps that had to be carried.

Two relevant points to note about these maps:
- The ½ Million shows **all** existing controlled airspace.
- The ¼ Million shows only controlled airspace from Surface to 5000 ft.

Should you choose to use the ¼ Million in the air you should still be in possession of the relevant ½ Million for planning purposes on the ground. There are other types of maps available but the above named two are sufficient for the time being.

Care of Maps

Ensure that any maps you choose have a glossy finish. This is essential to allow for the use of marker pens and subsequent erasure of any marks. The glossy finish also adds to the life span of the map protecting it from dirt and the elements.

If a particular map you require is not available in the glossy finish, a covering of clear 'fablon' will do the trick.

Whilst on the subject of protection, never leave your maps exposed to sunlight for any length of time. If you do, the colours will fade and important features such as hills and woods may not so easily be discerned.

Pre Flight Planning – Part 1

You plan to fly from A to B. Your first task is to draw in the Tr.Req. line on a ½ Million map and check for proximity to, or infringement of, controlled airspace and other 'taboo' zones.

Even if such zones encountered are only relevant above 3000 ft., you should check that any factors such as high ground will not force you to climb to such a height as to make such zones relevant. If so then you must adjust the track line accordingly.

Similarly, you have to avoid built up areas. Also, the code of the micro-light pilot demands that adequate landing ground is always ahead and below.

By now the Tr.Req. line may no longer be a straight line but consist of several 'legs'. At least you can rest content that your chosen path is a safe one.

Preparing a Flight Plan

Relying upon memory for a flight plan can be disastrous. Almost as bad, is scribbling pieces of vital information on a scrap of paper. The use of some planned type of form is highly recommended as reference to same in the air needs to be easy and instant.

The example below should provide some food for thought.

In the process of working out headings you will also be in possession of other data, such as your groundspeed in relation to your planned airspeed.

Knowing your groundspeed over each leg and the distance you have to cover, the time in air becomes a simple calculation allowing further planning.

(i)   Planned airspeed of 55 mph is calculated to give a 45 mph ground-speed

(ii) Total track to be flown is 80 miles which at 45 mph means—

$$\frac{\text{Track}}{\text{GS}} \text{ or } \frac{80}{45} = 1 \text{ hr } 47 \text{ mins flying time.}$$

(iii) Your fuel state allows for a cruise time of 1½ hours endurance which would take you—

GS × Endurance of 45 × 1½ = about 68 miles along track.

(iv) A re-fuelling stop is necessary after 50 or so miles have been covered. This is playing it on the safe side to allow for you having used more power than intended and to allow a reserve for finding and landing at that stop.

**MICROLIGHT AIRCRAFT
CROSS COUNTRY FLIGHT PLAN**

Date:	Route:		Height AMSL.
Name:	Out Landings:		
A/craft Type:	Reg. QNH.		
Reg. No.			

F/cast from:	Dir.	Vel.	Time of F/cast:			
Wind at 2,000 ft.			Turbulence	Vis.	Cloud/Base	
Est. for 1,000 ft.						
Est. for 500 ft.						

LEG	Tr. Req.	Est. Drift	Var.	Hdg. Mag.	G/S	ETA	Altim. Adj't.

NOTES: (Waypoints, Landmarks, High Ground, Etc.)

LEG	Tr. Req.	Est. Drift	Var.	Hdg. Mag.	G/S	ETA	Altim. Adj't.

NOTES: (Waypoints, Landmarks, High Ground, Etc.)

LEG	Tr. Req.	Est. Drift	Var.	Hdg. Mag.	G/S	ETA	Altim. Adj't.

NOTES: (Waypoints, Landmarks, High Ground, Etc.)

LEG	Tr. Req.	Est. Drift	Var.	Hdg. Mag.	G/S	ETA	Altim. Adj't.

NOTES: (Waypoints, Landmarks, High Ground, Etc.)

ALTIMETER SETTING FOR QFE AT DESTINATION
If no pressure setting scale, **set height amsl.** on take off. On arrival overhead, **reduce** altimeter reading
by the height amsl of destination to give a 0 ft. reading on landing (QFE).
E.g. Enstone 550' to Wellesbourne 160'. Set 550' on take off.
    Overhead Wellesbourne, reduce reading by 160'.
    On landing, altimeter reading will be 0' (QFE).

Pre Flight Planning – Part 2

Any scheduled re-fuelling stop must now be marked on the map with the nearest rather than the furthest suitable site being selected within the mileage range necessary.

The next step is to establish 'waypoints' on your Tr.Req. Waypoints are easily identifiable features marked at intervals on the map which when sighted confirm that you are on track or not as the case may be.

In the absence of a compass it is essential that they be close enough together for the next one to be in view from the present one.

At the outset and at every change of heading, double up on the waypoints you mark – later you will see the value of so doing.

For a few miles radius around your destination, ring that spot with additional marked features. You may assess that you have reached your journey's end to find that it is not there. Having made it thus far it is reasonable to assume that your goal cannot be far away. With your destination ringed with marked features within a **'circle of uncertainty'** you will be in a much better position to sort yourself out.

Should you have worked out your speeds accurately and feel that you can stick to them in the air then your waypoints can be fixed at regular time intervals of say 5 minutes flight duration between each. Here you have the advantage of checking the progress you are making in terms of ground-speed.

Reading the map in the air

How you secure your map in flight for easy reference is a matter for your own ingenuity and initiative. Some pilots like to have the map 'the right way up' – others like to orientate it so that they are flying along the track line with features coming up on the ground as they appear on the map. The choice is yours.

Having taken off, climb to a position central to your take-off point, which in essence is the start of your Tr.Req. line, and adopt your planned heading at the same time checking it for accuracy. This you do by positioning your aircraft so that the doubled up waypoints referred to earlier are in line with each other. Once this picture is set up check that your planned heading matches it – if not, adopt the new heading, make a note of it and stick to it for that leg.

You are now sure of being on your Tr.Req. and have allowed for any drift. Adopt the same procedure for each leg as a new heading becomes necessary.

Hints and Tips

Assuming you are now confidently on your way it is time to take note of a few hints and tips.

Waypoints   – Make sure the main selected waypoints marked on your map also take into account other features around them. It is no good spotting an 'expected' TV mast if it is the wrong one. Checking that those additional features are also present confirms your scheduled waypoint.

Again, if you spot an unexpected feature on your track which is not on your map – check the date of your map. New buildings and roads can appear quite quickly.

Features   – The higher you go the less obvious becomes that hill you find hard to struggle up on foot.

– Main roads which you know like the back of your hand as a motorist can be obscured from the air by foliage when lined with trees.

– Secondary roads with shallow hedging, or no hedging at all can easily be mistaken for main roads due to the clarity with which they stand out. This would particularly apply when over the Fenland.

– Railway lines across country are fine but close to a town they usually multiply and can lead to confusion.

– Dis-used railway lines are excellent as they are invariably untended and therefore stand out like scars in an otherwise orderly agricultural surround.

– Woods are very useful but the Forestry Commission do fell trees from time to time so ensure your map is up to date.

– Motorways, new by-passes and dual carriageways can quickly make a map out of date. Ensure you do not become confused at sighting newly constructed ones which are so prevalent around new towns.

Cloud Shadow – The shadow cast on the ground by a cloud can quickly obliterate that all important waypoint you expect to see come up on schedule. Cope with this by an intermediate check of features which should be around but not marked down during your preparation.

Sun   – The sun in your eyes, particularly on a hazy day, can play havoc with your forward visibility. Anticipate this possibility by increasing the number of marked waypoints before you start. This is also a good move for a hazy/misty day when the sun is not so dominant.

Sun Spots   – Far ahead you see your destination clearly basking in a pool of sunlight between shadows. If your concentration is not up to the mark you may find yourself heading for that pool of sunlight which will, of course, be moving away from your destination at the speed of the wind at cloud level.

By all means use the sighting far ahead but only to line up with a known waypoint to confirm your current heading or to initiate a change in same if it is warranted.

No doubt you will find out many other 'wrinkles' for yourself, proving that map reading is very much a practical art rather than a theoretical one.

Dealing with Problems

There are times when to be realistic about it, you come across problems. Your engine is playing up or for some other reason such as whether you cannot maintain your planned height and the possibility of a precautionary landing must be considered.

The lower you are the less time you have to select a field in the event of needing one. In this situation it is essential that you are governed by common sense and not a blind adherence to your planned track. Deviate from the track where necessary to ensure that any given moment you have a safe landing ground below you without having to rely on any normal gliding time to reach it. This is not to say that there is not a need to fly at all times with an unscheduled landing in mind. It is simply a matter of when the problem arises low down the choice is drastically reduced. Unscheduled landings need an assessment to be made of wind direction. It would be sad to 'bend' your aircraft through a crosswind touch-down when conditions were otherwise ideal.

Smoke has traditionally been the life saver in the past but today there is little of it about to show up a wind direction. One such aid can be ripples across water. A stretch of water sheltered by trees or a high bank at one end will show a calm patch of water at that sheltered end.

Cloud shadow moving across the ground is another aid, but remember to aim around 30° to the **left** of the shadow's track as you turn into wind – the shadow's movement will be more in line with the geostrophic wind direction than that of the surface wind.

All in all, your safest move is to monitor any indication of wind direction at intervals during the flight and not leave it until a problem arises.

Probably the greatest hazard you will ever have to face in landing out is that of power lines. The wires or cables themselves are unlikely to be seen until the last minute and certainly not from any reasonable height. However, the pylons or poles supporting them are certainly visible if you care to keep a careful look-out so whenever you see two poles always assume them to be joined by a cable.

Not to be recommended is flying under power lines, but in the course of driving about the countryside you should take note of the cable heights in relation to the types of pylons/poles in terms of size. There is more to be said for passing underneath than for stalling-in on the top of this hazard.

Finally, should you be lost, there is always the sun. If the time is around midday, drop down until your shadow is visible on the ground and with the knowledge that the sun will be to the south at that time you should be able to obtain a reasonable check on your heading. Shadow to right, you are going west; shadow to left, you are going east; shadow in front, you are going north. You should not need to be told in what direction you are heading when the sun is directly in front.

When lost in the proximity of controlled airspace unless you are quite sure that you can quickly re-establish your position in a very short space of time then land at once and find out exactly where you are. At least a microlight allows you this facility, denied to most other aviators, and it is better to be safe than sorry.

Map reading can be a very rewarding task. There is a tremendous satisfaction to be had as well as safety in knowing that you are where you planned to be at all times.

Index